arriving at amen

"Atheist convert Leah Libresco is well-known for her sharp mind, dogged curiosity, and fresh perspective on faith. *Arriving at Amen* puts those gifts on full display. Her reflections on prayer and the spiritual journey are brilliant, unique, and utterly refreshing. With this book, Leah hasn't just arrived at Amen; she's arrived as one of the premier young, Catholic writers today."

Brandon Vogt
Author of *Saints and Social Justice*

"At once a conversion story and a practical treatise of the exploration of prayer, *Arriving at Amen* is a surprising little gem of a book, so fresh and insightful that it belies Leah Libresco's status as a recent convert to Catholicism. *Arriving at Amen* literally made me gasp, because I suddenly realized I was holding a diamond; the most intellectually stimulating, humbling, and entertaining Catholic book I have read in a very, very long time."

Elizabeth Scalia
Catholic blogger and author of *Strange Gods*

"Direct, uncluttered, and full of spiritual insight, Leah Libresco's singularly helpful book is for anyone seeking a deeper and richer and more reflective life of faith."

R. R. Reno
Editor of *First Things*

"Leah Libresco's account of her journey of faith is a wonderful gift. Whether it's music or math, dancing or pottery, she uses personal experiences to show us how to develop a daily life of ever-deepening prayer. This book is a delight to read."

Scott Hahn
Bestselling author of *Angels and Saints*

"Reading Leah Libresco's book is like being taken on a tour of your hometown by a brilliant, quirky guide who helps you see everything anew. *Arriving at Amen* is a delightfully refreshing read that will help any Catholic see the Faith through new eyes."

Jennifer Fulwiler
Author of *Something Other Than God*

arriving at amen

Seven Catholic Prayers That Even I Can Offer

Leah Libresco

AVE MARIA PRESS AVE Notre Dame, Indiana

Unless otherwise noted, scripture quotations in this book are from the *New Revised Standard Version Bible: Catholic Edition*, © 1989, Division of Christian Education of the National Council of Churches of Christ in the U.S.A. Used by permission. All rights reserved.

Verses marked NKJV are from the *New King James Version*, © 1982 by Thomas Nelson Publishers. Used by permission. All rights reserved.

Verses marked KJV are from the *King James Version of the Bible*.

Verses marked DO are from the online breviary at DivineOffice.org.

Founded in 1865, Ave Maria Press is a ministry of the United States Province of Holy Cross.

www.avemariapress.com

Paperback: ISBN-13 978-1-59471-587-7

E-book: ISBN-13 978-1-59471-588-4

Cover and text design by Andy Wagoner.

Printed and bound in the United States of America.

Library of Congress Cataloging-in-Publication Data

Libresco, Leah.
  Arriving at amen : seven Catholic prayers that even I can offer / Leah Libresco.
    pages cm
  Includes bibliographical references.
  ISBN 978-1-59471-587-7 -- ISBN 1-59471-587-4
  1. Prayer--Catholic Church. I. Title.
  BV210.3.L53 2015
  248.3'2--dc23
                                2014049132

Contents

Foreword

This may sound strange coming from a Catholic apologist, but when atheist Leah Libresco announced that she was entering the Catholic Church, I felt vaguely let down. Atheism would no longer have Leah around to (as she sunnily puts it) "pick fights" on behalf of the No God crew. I knew the online conversation would again subside into the normal boring round of Flying Spaghetti Monster chatter and "If God created everything, then who created God?" high school sophomore philosophy that Libresco-less atheism tended to comprise. I would miss her Ideological Turing Tests, in which she challenged believers and nonbelievers to do their level best to get into each other's heads rather than simply caricature each other's positions. I would miss her "geek orthodox" analogies from gamer culture, math, and sci-fi/fantasy. I would miss her cheery, friendly confidence that the Truth would not lie to her and her willingness to follow an argument wherever it led. I would miss her ability to call out intellectual laziness (mine as much as anybody else's) in atheist/believer arguments. In short, I would miss her old-school belief that the purpose of arguing was not to win but to clarify.

I am happy to report that I didn't wind up missing any of Leah's rhetorical energy for long, since she brought it all with her into the Church, verifying once again Saint Thomas Aquinas's conviction that grace perfects rather than destroys nature. It is in Leah's nature—whether as an atheist or as a believer—to be a highly original thinker, and therefore to restate old truth (and all truth is old) in fresh ways. You hold in your hands the proof of this statement.

Leah's great gift is that she really, really trusts the Truth. She trusts not only that (in the words of *The X-Files*) the Truth Is Out There (sometimes Way Out There, as the astonishing Truth of the Incarnation, Death, and Resurrection of God Almighty demonstrates), but that the Truth is also In Here: in our intimate communion via the Holy Spirit with the Immanent God, who speaks to us through our personal struggles, questions, confusions, and crazy intuitions as we examine them in light of apostolic tradition.

In pursuing the Truth, Leah is (rather like the apostles were) unafraid to say, "I don't get it," and to propose her questions and judgments about life, the universe, and everything to Jesus and his Church. She is not rude in her questioning, or defiant or impious. Rather, she wrestles with God like the patriarch Jacob. In her clear-headed way, she asks things that the rest of us are too timid to ask—yielding answers from Christ that the rest of us are too timid to get.

After all, who hasn't thought, "Why am I asking God for stuff he already knows I need?" or, "Isn't it silly to demand that justice be meted out to bad guys but I get mercy for me?" Leah is willing to tough it out and stay with those kinds of questions until she receives an answer that satisfies—one that does not bend or mutilate either sacred tradition or the interior apprehension of truth, mercy, and justice put into our hearts by God. She believes—believed even before her conversion—that we shall know the Truth, and the Truth will make us free (Jn 8:32).

The originality—and, in a funny way, charity—of Leah's thought is nowhere better on display than in the introduction of this book, wherein she extols the virtues of one of the most unlikeable characters in all of world literature: the entirely uncharitable Inspector Javert of *Les Misérables*. Through Leah's eyes, we see how this creature of rules and regulations—of self-sufficiency and inflexible, merciless rectitude—is attempting (as we all do) to reach a good end but by bad and ultimately self-destructive means. More than this, we see this merciless man through the eyes of God's (and Leah's) mercy. Who but Leah Libresco would begin a book on prayer by referring us to so unyielding and adamant a character—and find her way through him to the ever-beckoning God of mercy, of grace, and, yes, of answer to prayer?

Who but Leah Libresco could formulate the completely original yet old-as-the-gospel discovery that "I guess morality just loves me or something" and the realization that "morality wasn't just a rulebook, but some kind of agent" who had leapt to her across the chasm that she could not cross herself? She may not have known it when she first had these insights, but they are as serviceable a restatement of John 1:1–14 ("In the beginning was the Word. . . . And the Word became flesh and lived among us. . . .") as you could ask for. It is characteristic of her sense of intellectual freedom—a deeply Catholic sense—that she would come to the Truth of Christ. This is somebody who, under the grace of the Holy Spirit, really thinks, and so it is no surprise that she has come to think with the mind of Christ, who is the Power and Wisdom of God.

What I appreciate most about Leah's work in this book is that it shows how deeply humane and full of charity she is. Just as she appreciates the finer qualities of even a merciless Javert, she approaches even her enemies with the mercy of Christ—and is, paradoxically, merciless with her own falsities, charades, self-flatteries, flummery, and balderdash as she does so. For she came to realize that we are all in Javert's boat, only not quite so stony as he in our refusals of grace. Here we can see that Leah's own atheist past, under the guidance of God's strange grace, taught her well. She grew up as a sort of Stoic: wanting to do and think and say the right and the true and the good, not for the sake of reward, but purely for the sake of virtue. Where most people fear lack of popularity, she feared flattery and being told what she wanted to hear. In consequence, when she did hear the Good News, she really heard it and took it in, not because it promised her health or wealth or fame or power or honor or pie in the sky when she dies by and by, but because Jesus is what she had been seeking: Goodness, Reality, and Beauty or, as he himself put it, the Way, the Truth, and the Life.

Not, of course, that she doesn't struggle. This book is a chronicle of struggles, questions, confusions—and spiritual progress under grace. Indeed, one of its greatest merits is that Leah, by her own free admission, does not have it together when it comes to prayer. She struggles to arrive at "Amen." But then, so do we all. As Saint Paul notes in Romans 8:26, "we do not know how to pray as we ought," and this fact marks Leah's experience of prayer as well. She both relies on and struggles with the many helps and graces Christ gives to us through his teaching, his inspired word in scripture, his

Church, the liturgy, the saints, and the abundance of other ways his Spirit pours out grace on us.

In this book, Leah does us the great favor, not of being a spiritual master, but rather of being a fellow kindergartner with us, jumping up and down excitedly when she finds something new and beautiful. Join her on her journey into prayer, and you will find your prayer life kindled anew.

Mark P. Shea
Author of *By What Authority?*

Introduction
Chasing Truth as Javert Does

I've wanted to be a lot of things when I grew up. When I was four years old, I told my preschool teacher that I wanted to be Supergirl. On and off, I've wanted to follow in my parents' footsteps and be a teacher. When I was in college, after reading through a slew of badly designed research abstracts, I wanted to be a methodology cop; I wanted to carry a badge, kick in doors, and put a stop to poorly conceived studies before they had the chance to waste anyone's time. But the most transfixing sense of who I wanted to be when I grew up came to me during middle school when my family went to see the musical *Les Misérables*.

I didn't fall in love with tragic Éponine or fearless Enjolras or noble Jean Valjean, but with Javert, the story's antagonist. Police Inspector Javert relentlessly pursues Jean Valjean, the story's protagonist, who at the beginning of the show has just finished serving a sentence of nineteen years' hard labor for stealing a loaf of bread. Once he discovers that no one will hire or shelter an ex-con, Valjean breaks his parole and forges new identity papers. Inspector Javert swears to find Valjean and bring him to justice.

A Hymn to Order and Duty

Javert appears in the opening number, but for a long time afterwards he is absent, only an implicit threat. When he finally catches up with Valjean by chance, he swiftly loses him again. Alone on the stage, Javert sings his first solo, "Stars," a hymn to order and duty. Javert doesn't hate Valjean or love glory; he sees himself as the steadfast servant of order. Although Valjean is the character who goes through a Christian resurrection through sacrifice and forgiveness, Inspector Javert prays, too: he prays for the chance to serve God by preserving his law.

At the time I did not believe in God, but as I listened to "Stars" I wanted nothing so much as to grow up to resemble Javert. I wanted to grow up to be just that tall, stable, ramrod-straight, inviolate, and wholly consecrated to duty. I didn't understand why, at intermission, no one else's eyes were shining the way mine were when we talked about the unrelenting officer.

Javert is untouchable and uncompromising. Because he loves the law above all other things, even himself, he is free from fear and corruption. Later in the show, he is captured by the student revolutionaries and held prisoner at their barricade. Even when they threaten him, there's a kind of joy in his voice when he sings,

> Shoot me now or shoot me later
> Every schoolboy to his sport
> Death to each and every traitor
> I renounce your people's court![1]

It's the exhilaration of someone who has loyally stood by his dearest love, no matter what threats were brought to bear. I was on the edge of my seat, proud of him, wishing for the power to keep my promises the way Javert did.

Inspector Javert doesn't wind up martyred by the students for the sake of the rule of law because Valjean, his quarry, finds Javert and releases him from the barricade. Javert, so committed to the law that he cannot comprehend mercy, is caught in a paradox of duty. He would betray his oath as a policeman if he allowed Valjean to go free, but he would betray his debt to Valjean if he arrested him. Unable to neglect either duty, Javert commits suicide, wronging only himself to avoid failing in duty.

When I was older, I turned to the Victor Hugo novel on which the musical was based and found the same unrelenting fairness I had loved in song laid out in prose. In the book, Valjean breaks his parole and changes his name, eventually becoming the much-beloved mayor of a town. Javert is assigned to the same town, grows suspicious, and reports Valjean to the authorities. However, he comes to believe he has misidentified Valjean and goes to the disguised mayor to apologize and receive his just punishment—but not to ask for forgiveness or mercy:

> In my life, I have often been severe toward others. It was just. I was right. Now if I were not severe toward myself, all I have justly done would become injustice. Should I spare myself more than others? No. You see! If I had been eager only to punish others and not myself, that would have been despicable. Those who say, "That scoundrel Javert" would have been right. Monsieur Mayor, I do not wish you to treat me with kindness. Your kindness, when it was for others, enraged

> me quite enough; I do not wish it for myself. . . .
> Such kindness disorganizes society. Good God,
> it is easy to be kind, the difficulty is being just.[2]

If Javert were simply cruel or malicious, he would not have presented himself for punishment when he erred. He serves the law, not his own self-interest. Because Javert stubbornly refuses to accept mercy himself, he feels he has license to deny it to everyone else. After all, he never holds anyone to a standard higher than that to which he holds himself.

Mistrusting Mercy

As a child until nearly the present day, I shared Javert's suspicion of kindness. It seemed horribly condescending to me for friends or family to refuse to acknowledge a wrong as wrong or to pretend it was all right for me to have consented to it. It made no more sense to me than marking a wrong answer on math homework as correct. Those who ignored or minimized wrong behavior, I thought, must assume that their friends *couldn't* improve themselves—so there was no sense in upsetting them by pointing out that they'd fallen short of the mark. I found this assumption insulting.

Since I couldn't trust other people to police my actions adequately, I tried to do it myself. If I was late for a class, I would solemnly tell my teacher why and then note, "But that is an explanation, not an excuse." As an atheist, I didn't believe in any kind of moral anti-entropic force that would or could pull me out of an immoral rut. The only anti-corrupting force I could trust in was myself—my own efforts and conscientiousness.

Just as Javert carefully policed the boundaries of the law he loved, I took joy in following rules carefully; however, in the process I turned kindness into a competitive zero-sum game, in which giving kindness cancelled out receiving it. I wanted to do my duty so completely as to never be indebted to anyone else. I remembered Linus Pauling's advice to "do unto others twenty percent better than you would expect them to do unto you, to correct for subjective error." If something seemed "fair" to me, I assumed I was rationalizing, that the status quo was probably slightly biased in my favor.

The more unpleasant a duty, the more delight I took in fulfilling it. If my teachers thought I was unusually patient when a troop of bullies chose me as a target, they missed the way I relished the taunts, just for the pleasure of not rising to the bait and being able to add one more act to my tally of "right choices." I treated moral excellence like academic achievement—I wanted to tackle the hardest moral dilemmas I could handle, ace them, and move on to the next challenge.

By the time I got to high school, it was more impressive to say that my commitment to duty over sentiment was guided by Immanuel Kant and his categorical imperative than to refer to a fictional, singing antihero, but I idolized the two in tandem. Kant warned his readers that they should be attached to duty for the sake of duty alone, not for any other internal or external reward. The ideal thing, it seemed to me, would be to do the correct thing always and always to be despised for it, so that my choices would be entirely untainted by rewards from others. (This disposition helped me enjoy high school a good deal more than the average person.)

Before I ever assented to Christianity, I conceded that, within its standards, Javert is a heretic, not a saint. He (and I) weren't even particularly unique or dashing heretics. Javert fits squarely into the mold of a Pelagian—someone who, by appropriating all the work of salvation for himself, preempts the role of God's grace.

That seemed all right to me. Like Javert, I sensed *cheating* in the Christian story of an infinitely forgiving God. I wanted to rise only as high as I could manage with my own efforts rather than have my devotion to duty swamped by the overwhelming power of a god's help, if such a being existed.

After all, the moral law clearly existed outside of me and would go on existing without me. My job was simply to measure up. To imply that the law would or could flex to help me was as silly as saying that my measuring tape, in a spirit of sympathy with my desire to be taller, would willfully contract itself in order to eke out the extra inch to make me five foot seven. Once the measure of length had compromised itself in order to "help" me, it forfeited its integrity as a measure.

The Price of an Intelligible Universe

My appreciation for order and regularity, even if it inconvenienced me, meant I never had much trouble with one of the main traditional objections to Christianity (or any religion that posits a loving God): the problem of evil—the question of how any pain and suffering could be countenanced by an all-powerful, all-good God.

Consider the simpler problem of natural evils and accidents (falling masonry, flooding, car crashes, virulent flus, etc.). For God to deliver us from all natural pains, the laws of physics would have to be studded with asterisks specifying all the times that flying, twisted metal would need to flout the conservation of linear momentum to stop just short of breaking our bones.

I knew what such a world would look like, for it had already been imagined in the sagas of Norse mythology. In one legend, the godling Baldr prophesies his own death, and all the other gods of the Norse pantheon try to save him. The gods and goddesses of Asgard travel the world, extracting a vow from every natural and created thing, be it, bird, plant, stone, or sword, never to do Baldr any harm. Once his safety is secured, the Asgardians amuse themselves at feasts by throwing knives and other weapons at Baldr, in order to watch the objects keep their promises, defy their natures, and leave him unhurt. Blades blunt themselves, stones soften, and poison neutralizes itself, all to avoid inflicting any pain on Baldr.

To preclude the problem of evil, it seemed, any god would have to give us the same guarantee afforded Baldr. The world around us would have to warp itself to shield us from the weather, from accidents, from gravity, until the laws of physics were unworthy of the name. There couldn't be scientists or empiricism in this kind of world, since the nature of matter would be too protean for us to gain intellectual purchase on.

The problem of evil has always seemed to me to be the price we pay for having an intelligible world, one that we can investigate, understand, and love. If miracles were to be possible, they would have to stay below some threshold level of frequency so that they remained clear exceptions to the general course of causality (as in the case of poor, strange Baldr) instead of undoing the rule entirely.

It is the regularity of the world that allows us to struggle toward some understanding of it. Most science has progressed by building a model of the world and then checking the model to see if there are any circumstances in which it fails. Inductive learning depends on the assumption that dropping a stone and a feather tomorrow will yield the same results as dropping them today—that the laws of physics won't have rewritten themselves overnight.

But this regularity is not the only assumption we rely on in order to grow in our understanding of the world. We also need to have feedback loops, the ability to receive information about the consequences of our actions. Dropping the stone and the feather with my eyes closed wouldn't advance my understanding of gravity; I have to watch the speed at which they fall. Very few people doubt that we can create these kinds of feedback loops to learn about the physical laws of nature, even if we sometimes need a microscope to augment our eyes or a particle accelerator to generate the phenomena we want to see.

Collecting and learning from data becomes more complicated when we want to investigate moral or mathematical laws, which can't be derived simply by observing physical phenomena. Experimental philosophers such as Kwame Anthony Appiah and Jonathan Haidt generate data by posing hypothetical scenarios to survey subjects and tweaking the conditions of the dilemma to discover what influences people's moral reasoning. ("Would you kill one man to be able to use his organs to save five other patients?" "Would you condone incestuous sex if it happened only once, and both partners were already sterile?")

However, this kind of research into morality tells us more about human psychology than about moral law. A descriptive survey of our current moral intuitions doesn't tell us anything about what moral feelings we ought to follow. When researchers discover that people are more willing to sacrifice others for the greater good when they are asked in a second language to do so than they are when asked in their native tongue, the scientists are teasing out something more akin to a cognitive bias than a better understanding of morals.

Treating Morals like Math

Philosophers who study ethics, rather than people's thoughts about ethics, tend to look a little more like Kant or Aquinas—people who lay out their core assumptions about what is good and see what follows from them. That is to say, they look a lot like mathematicians. They retreat to their surest axioms and build out theorems from that foundation. But mathematicians themselves are split on whether this mode of inquiry is related to some deeper truth or whether it is just an exercise in imagination.

Some mathematicians are *nominalists*, who don't believe that mathematics describes any higher, abstract truth. In their view, mathematicians are like novelists, who are constrained by the rules they create but whose discipline doesn't reveal anything transcendentally true.

Even Javert could be a nominalist. If he has one unshakeable axiom, it is that the laws of France are worth enforcing, but he may love them simply because they are orderly and constant, rather than for any particular content they carry. (Hugo's book leaves open the possibility that Javert is an atheist.) Javert may, like some mathematicians, acknowledge that the rules he enforces are arbitrary but follow them to their logical conclusions as an intellectual discipline.

Other mathematicians fall into the category of *Platonists*, believing that math existed prior to humans and that we can trace out the rules and perfections that are already written, but that we cannot add to them by making up arbitrary new axioms and treating those as equally interesting. Under this model, it's not enough just to pick *a* rule and apply it fairly and consistently. Some starting principles are better than others, since those axioms, when combined with the right rules for induction, will actually lead you to better understand the world.

The mathematics principles beloved by the Platonists may seem abstract, but luckily for us, the airy realm of math seems to inform our quotidian realm. Math is written into the world around us, so that even supposedly theoretical fields of inquiry keep manifesting as patterns in the natural world. At this point, many mathematicians would be surprised to discover any particularly beautiful theorem that isn't somehow, somewhere, manifested in the physical world.

Today's moral philosophers don't get taken as seriously when they make similar Platonic claims. As I got drawn into more arguments with friends who were moral relativists, I couldn't point to anything in the world that firmly embodies moral truths the way the seeds of a sunflower incarnate the Fibonacci sequence. I didn't take any pleasure or see any hope in being a creature of duty who served the arbitrary rules of nominalism, but my friends saw me that way—they didn't think I had much cause to claim that my actions were informed by anything other than my own arbitrary preferences and prejudices.

It was true, they conceded, that they themselves acted as though their own moral judgments were related to some kind of moral law, but they didn't have *my* arrogance to claim this was because they actually were following something transcendent. There was nothing objective to measure moral claims against, they said: no real science of ethics, just the study of the psychology of our attachment to the idea of ethics.

What Calibrates a Conscience?

Every fiber of my being rebelled against this assertion. To me, dismissing our consciences as compasses because we are as yet unable to dissect them satisfactorily and because they are sometimes biased seemed as ridiculous as pooh-poohing the existence and accuracy of sight in the years before we had dissected the eye. After all, the process of seeing was mysterious and clearly prone to error and confusion in the form of optical illusions, but we could see quite reliably before we'd learned how pictures of the world arrived in our heads physically.

However, I had to concede that part of my analogy didn't quite hold up. The eye makes visual sense of the physical world, but I hadn't quite defined what the conscience was "seeing" and interpreting. If I wanted to describe the conscience as a sense, I needed to figure out what it perceived, and some kind of Platonic rulebook wasn't quite the answer.

We didn't come to understand the laws of physics or mathematics by just contemplating abstraction; we had to bootstrap our way there by studying the world around us, looking at shapes and movement, and taking our first steps into abstraction as we began to spot patterns. In Plato's terms, we come to understand forms by seeing them as points of commonality between the otherwise unrelated physical phenomena around us. We watch an apple, a twig, and ourselves fall and begin to sketch out gravity as the force that seizes hold of all these distinct objects. We see an orange, a stone polished by the river, and the sun and develop an idea of roundness as the category that unites all these objects.

I couldn't quite sketch out the same kind of progression to describe how we came to understand moral laws and regularities. On the night of my conversion, I had been drawn into this same argument with a Lutheran friend and was rehearsing again why I couldn't confidently claim that we developed our moral sense by watching a person pinch an infant and another person kick a dog, and uniting both actions under the heading of "cruelty."

"Well, if that's not your answer, how do we know?" my friend asked. "If you've already thrown that one out, there's not that much point in repeating it."

I was stuck.

By itself, being stuck wasn't enough reason to change my mind. After all, I was twenty-three, so my not having personally worked it out yet was hardly an indication that a problem was unsolvable. I was a little exhilarated by the problem, and I hoped to be of use to my fellow atheists by shoring up our defense against one of the best points our opponents had on us.

My friend's pointed, unanswered question wasn't, as far as I could tell, a fatal blow—it was better to admit honestly that your model of the world was incomplete than to paper over the gap with "God"—but I couldn't understand why more of my atheist friends and the atheist writers I read weren't interested in explaining how we receive access to moral law.

Prodded by my friend, I tried to at least do something new in this argument, rather than rehash old ideas. Stepping back from focusing on the gap in my understanding of the world, I considered my whole chain of reasoning, to see if I'd be better off approaching my confusion a different way. I wanted a chance to notice if one of my premises was faulty.

A Proof by Contradiction

Mathematicians sometimes come to the truth via *proofs by contradiction*. Usually, when they're using this technique deliberately, they assume the opposite of the theorem they're trying to prove and trace out its logical consequences until they contradict something that we all know to be true (something as obvious as two plus two equals four). Since we have a great deal more confidence in the sum of two and two than in the antitheorem that contradicted it, the antitheorem gets thrown out as false, proving that the theorem is true.

Sometimes, though, mathematicians wind up using this kind of proof accidentally. A perfectly ordinary proof suddenly turns absurd, and the poor scholar has to go back through it, line by line, to discover where a false premise snuck in. When your answer doesn't make sense, you find whatever premise you're least sure of and try discarding it.

Finding myself stuck, I turned to this latter approach; these were the basic things I turned out to believe (my premises):

    a. There probably isn't a God.

    b. Some things are right and some things are wrong, even if everyone on Earth is mistaken about which is which.

    c. I (and everyone else) have some level of access to these moral truths, even if I don't directly know the rules on which they depend.

    d. Starting just from reason and the physical world, I can't naturally learn the laws of ethics the way I can the laws of physics.

I summarized my reasoning to my interlocutor, and he pushed again: "Well, then what?"

"I don't know," I said. "Somehow we get across the gap of abstraction, but not by a process I currently understand. I just know *a* solution exists, since I do in fact have access (however imperfect) to moral reasoning."

"Right, but how?"

"I don't know, I guess morality just loves me or something."

We both fell silent. I asked my friend to stay quiet while I figured out whether I actually believed what I'd just said. I'd always thought of morality as a set of static operating instructions for ethical actions, but if I had just conceded that moral reasoning and I were on opposite sides of a chasm that I couldn't bridge on my own, then I must believe that contact was made from the other side. Morality wasn't just a rulebook but some kind of agent.

But when I'd blurted my best guess, I hadn't said that morality merely reached me, as I might have if I were just picturing something like a giant, ambulatory grimoire. I had said "loves." I had spent too long thinking of moral law as analogous to mathematics—perfect, complete, independent—to imagine that it could *need* me. If morality reached out to me, it had to be offering itself as a gift: it wanted good *for* me, not *from* me.

What's more, it was hard to imagine imbuing the literal definition of Goodness with an active spirit and not finding that spirit to be good itself. Anything else would be as illogical as having the Spirit of Mathematics (if it existed) be innumerate.

I'd backed myself into a corner. There wasn't anyone else in the world who talked about "the Platonic ideal of the Good as an active agent with a special care for humankind" without shortening that whole cumbersome phrase to simply *God*.

Making Peace with Mercy

In the end, the nonexistence of God was the premise I was least sure of, and my firm belief in the law led (in a perfectly orderly way) to evidence for a lawmaker who was himself firmly on the side of disorderly mercy. Morality wasn't going to deceive me or pretend I measured up. It—which is to say God—was properly keeping track of my shortcomings, but its purpose was to know what in me still needed to be mended, not to dock me points on some great exam.

Having an ally in my project of following moral law was new and disconcerting. The mere fact that morality had made itself known to me, with the initiative all on God's side, was enough to make me a little uncomfortable. Javert might have resisted being handed the answers, unwilling to accept help he could not earn, but I had just enough love in me to be able to feel warmly surprised to find out the rules I loved, loved me back.

Figuring out how to live with this new ally was the work of more than an evening. In the months that followed, while I received instruction in the Catholic faith, I struggled to think of God as a person since I had spent so long thinking only about rules and regularity. In those moments when it felt more natural to think about math and theorems, I tried to use even those distractions as a way to open myself back up to God in prayer.

If I delighted in mathematics, that delight must in some way reflect God's own delight in what he had made. Math was something I could look at with God, my new ally, confident we were sharing our feeling of finding it good. And if God found joy in math, which was beautiful but inert, how must he feel about me, who was beginning (if haltingly) to be able to notice and share his joy?

But all those first, awkward, improvisational prayers were still a long way away on that night before Palm Sunday. That night, after I let go of my faulty premise and welcomed Christ into my heart, my Lutheran friend suggested we pray the Divine Office in celebration. It was the first of many times that I would rely on traditional Christian prayer practices to teach me the rules of the new world I had found myself in and, little by little, open my heart to grace.

Chapter 1
Petition

Petition may be the most common kind of prayer, but before my conversion, it was the kind I found the strangest. The Mass, with its otherworldly Eucharist, was eldritch enough to seem worth doing (if Christianity were true), but simple complaining didn't seem worthy of the name of prayer. Even if I conceded the existence of an omnipotent, omniscient, and omnibenevolent being, that second "omni" seemed enough to guarantee that the whole project was futile.

An omniscient God must know before I did what I wanted (and whether I should have it). I hated people cluttering up my time and attention to inform me of what I already knew. Petitionary prayer seemed to include every annoyance of Twitter or Instagram—an endless litany of whatever triviality happened to pop into everyone's head. I couldn't imagine inflicting this kind of prayer upon the all-knowing God.

Tattling to God

Considering my attitude toward this prayer practice, it is not surprising that the superfluity or necessity of petitionary prayer was a matter of dispute between me and the Catholic boy I dated in college. The dispute remained mostly abstract until I got into a fairly nasty, personal fight with one of the other people running my debate group. A classmate who is not named Madison had made some accusations, in front of everyone, that weren't true and that really upset me. I held it together at our meetings but kept bursting into tears when I was alone with my boyfriend. He would comfort me and help me manage the fallout among our friends; finally, he added that he was going to pray for Madison and that I was welcome to join in, if I liked.

I spat back something like, "I'm not going to *tattle* on Madison to God! And I wouldn't ask any kind of god to change her just because I'm too weak to deal with her without getting upset. If I were going to pray for anything, I'd only be praying to handle this better. Or not to be so stupid as to leave her or anyone else an opening next time!"

Stoicism and Kantianism had both taught me that I shouldn't care too much what other people thought of me or how they treated me. The Stoics would have said that Madison's response wasn't under my control, so it was as useless to be upset that she was being mean to me as it would to be upset that I got wet in the rain. In a storm or in an argument, my misery was my choice, something I opted to add to the experience of being wet (or slandered). And being upset did nothing to help, so it was an unworthy, self-harming choice.

Kant might have chimed in that I should focus on what *was* under my control—whether I was fulfilling my moral obligations toward Madison (not retaliating in anger, trying to find a fair solution, etc.), regardless of whether she was fulfilling her duties toward me. In fact, if she was treating me badly and making it harder to do what I ought, so much the better. It's easy to be nice to people who are nice to you, so there's not much credit in it, according to Kant. You might be doing the right thing because you expect your kindness to be reciprocated instead of doing it out of pure, abstract love for the duty itself.

My boyfriend's suggestion that I ask God for help was unthinkable in my worldview—even if I hadn't been an atheist at the time. He was suggesting I cheat rather than simply do what I ought. He was proposing that I ask God to change the situation to make my duty pleasurable because I was too weakly committed to the Good to pursue it for its own sake.

I explained all this to him, and he replied, "No, I wanted you to pray for *Madison* because it must be hard for Madison to be this angry at you. She's really furious, and this isn't even the first time this semester that she's flown off the handle, so it must be exhausting and frightening for Madison to reflexively respond this way to a disagreement that's as low stakes as this one."

Seeking the Good of the Other

I hadn't thought about our struggle this way before. I tended to treat other people's temperaments as immutable and mostly irrelevant since it wasn't (in Stoic terms) within my power to alter them. Since the other person's character was outside my control, I didn't give it much consideration when I was trying to figure out the right thing for me to do. I see now that I was behaving like a solipsist—as though I were the only real person in the world—since I barely cared whether I was interacting with real people or simulacra as long as I was giving the morally correct reaction to their actions.

But my boyfriend's comment made me pause and consider that what was best for Madison might be bigger than just

my doing my duty by her. Instead of imagining Madison and
her anger as inseparable, I supposed that there might be some
kind of authentic ur-Madison, just as literary scholars discuss
the existence of an ur-Hamlet, the original source for Shakespeare's text. I could imagine a Madison who was happiest
and freest and most herself. I could have sympathy for that
ur-Madison and imagine that she might feel slightly fright-
ened or trapped by the strength of her anger. My boyfriend
probably felt the same kind of sympathy for the ur-Leah he
envisioned, hampered and blinded by layers of briskness and
callousness.

If that kind of inner self was what God saw and loved—
the part of ourselves that was oppressed by sin, not melded
into it—it made more sense to me that there was a kind of
petition that wasn't just the equivalent of radioing in spiritual airstrikes to support you in a fight. Rather than calling
on God to take my side and make things easier on me or to
actively side *against* Madison and punish her, I could ask God
to help me fight *for* Madison and to help her fight *for* me, too.

Both of us were hobbled by faults—there was anger and
fear and callousness on both sides—and we both had the
option to want to be freed from slavery to those faults. If we
noticed that our positions were symmetrical, we also had the
chance to hope that freedom from spite, anxiety, and unchar-
ity would be offered to our erstwhile antagonist.

If we did so, we were conforming our wills to God's, not
just through negatively framed requests—asking to be purged
of sin—but by asking to be filled with and changed by the
love that God bears for us and for our former enemy. The act
of prayer would start that transformation, since prayer gives

me one small change to make: to assent to a desire of God's that I didn't always share.

Of course, at the time, I still didn't believe in God, so I didn't pray for Madison. I did try to be kinder and to treat her like a person instead of a bonus round in my own moral development; but for the most part, the whole exchange stayed an interesting academic point about theology in which I learned that petitionary prayer wasn't as silly as I thought. I tried to carry over the solidarity with people's best selves that I admired in my boyfriend's prayer into my secular life.

Thinking about petitionary prayer, in the midst of that fight and other conflicts that followed, gave me a sense of what it would be to look at other people and myself *sub specie aeternitatis*, from the perspective of eternity. From that God's-eye view, Madison's anger and my coldness were distorting the larger and lovelier people we were meant to be.

I came to realize that my petitionary prayer, although rooted in the specific troubles of my daily life, helped me redirect my gaze and approximate God's gaze. When I struggle with someone else, I can see through petitionary prayer that I am not locked directly in battle with them. I'm usually blundering around in the darkness that clouds their own light or letting my own imperfections blind me to the love they're offering me. I no longer seek to be farther away from them, so that we stop interfering with each other; I want to see them more clearly, so that we can rejoice in each other's ur-selves.

Ultimately, I don't want God to make me *safe* from an antagonist (or the antagonist from me), but to make me one with my former enemy. I have to be one with my enemy if I want to be one with Christ. He will never sunder himself from my opponent, so if I want to be incorporated into him, I can't nurse division or distance from someone who is currently frustrating me.

Fictional Characters as Intercessory Icons

I could assent to this theology in theory, but it was still hard for me to be moved to pray for the specific people from whom I was dividing myself. As I started trying to offer prayers of intercession, I was much more likely to have a spontaneous impulse to pray for fictional characters than for the people in my real life. Reading novels or watching movies and musicals tends to stir up more of a swelling in my heart and an empathetic desire to serve than does the bustle of everyday life.

For one thing, I still don't have very much practice thinking of prayer as an option in everyday life. When I run into interpersonal problems, I'm still busy exploring all my old habits and patterns, and it takes a conscious, deliberate effort for me to incorporate new responses I'm learning. And even when I remember that I can pray in the middle of a normal interaction, the logistics are not always clear to me in my overcrowded life. Do I want to just silently toss up a fast, declarative "Oh dear. Prayers for [this person]"? Do I want to extract myself from the conversation to wander off and pray out loud and in a way that will take more than fifteen seconds? Do I want to memorize or otherwise record the prayer intention and try to remember to come back to it later?

When I'm enjoying art, I'm more relaxed, less frenetic, and freer to quietly turn to God. I can't interrupt or inconvenience anyone else by praying while I'm reading, so it's easier to get into the habit of ejaculatory prayer whenever I'm swept up in a strong movement toward love.

It's always been easier for me respond with spontaneous, deep love to the struggles of fictional characters than it is for me to respond that way to real people—and that's not entirely due to a defect in my nature. Reading often affords me the benefit of third-person omniscient perspective to peer into the heads of all the characters, antagonists included. My empathy is seldom that active or accurate in real life.

Even in a book using a third-person limited perspective, where the characters aren't completely open for my inspection, the absence of an "I" still helps. Third-person limited perspective forces a kind of equality between the protagonist and the people he or she encounters, since they're all described from the outside.

Reading makes it easier for me to understand the internal logic of someone's actions. If I am drawn into a conflict in my day-to-day life, there is no exposition or soliloquy to show me what my antagonist is actually upset about or which of my actions rankles him or why he feels under threat. In books, it's easier to see that all human actions are, as Aristotle argues in the *Nicomachean Ethics*, aimed at some perceived good, even if it's a lesser good or an evil mistaken for a good.

I try to believe that this movement toward goodness is active in everyone I come into contact with, but I can't always see it in the course of normal life. Fiction helps me overcome my doubts by offering me a proof of concept, just as Christ remedied the skepticism of the apostle Thomas by showing him his wounds. However, when I return to the real world and try to move toward love without being able to peek at people's internal monologue, I can understand how great a blessing it would be to be one of "those who have not seen and yet have believed" (Jn 20:29, NKJV).

Of course, I don't want to grow too reliant on the insight that fiction gives me, but it's helpful to have *any* sphere of my life where prayer feels natural. Praying for fictional characters begins to transform prayer from a theological topic I read about, or even something I do on a schedule, to a practice that permeates my life and isn't confined by time or place. Encouraging any opportunity for prayer takes me a little closer to the exhortation Paul offers in his first letter to the Thessalonians: "Rejoice always, pray without ceasing, give thanks in all circumstances; for this is the will of God in Christ Jesus for you" (1 Thes 5:16–18).

Even if I were to make no effort to cultivate prayer for real people, I expect that nurturing these prayers for fictional people would cause the good habit to bleed over into other parts of my life. The habit of prayer anywhere helps create an affordance, an expectation that prayer is a possibility at any place and time.

But I have tried to speed the process along. When I pray for fictional characters, I sometimes try to offer those prayers in the same spirit as the general intercessions offered at Mass or the laments and pleas of the psalms. If I pray for Javert from *Les Misérables*, because his love of righteousness is so tinged with fear and defensiveness that he must doubt either the power or the goodness of God, I try to use him as an icon of all the people who also struggle with this very Pelagian weakness (me included). Javert gives me one specific, vivid example to hold in my mind and prompts me to pray for a broad class of people like him, even if no particular person comes to mind.

The intimacy of fiction helps me get to the point where, as the characters in *Les Misérables* sing, "to love another person is to see the face of God."[1] Praying for fictional characters draws my attention up to God by encouraging me to engage in spontaneous petitions, but it frequently also redirects my attention to the needs of the characters in my real life. Sometimes I recognize some aspect of a friend (or myself) in print and find I have much more empathy with the fictional doppelgänger than I did in the moment for the real person. I then have the chance to use my empathy with the fictional person as a kind of pilot line for my empathy with the real-world counterpart.

A pilot line is the first wire strung across a chasm that will eventually be spanned by a suspension bridge. It doesn't have to be very strong: the pilot line for the suspension bridge over Niagara Falls was a kite string, lofted across the gap and then secured at both ends. The pilot line only has to be strong enough to bear the weight of a second, stronger wire, which then supports the next cord, and so on until eventually the engineers are putting the final steel cables in place.

Feeling drawn to pray for a fictional character is enough of a pilot line to pull me into praying that God will lead me into the same love for a friend as I have for that character. This kind of prayer gives me a way to admit that I truly *would* like to return to unity and love with the person I'm frustrated with, even if at the moment I need to stand at the remove of an analogy to admit it.

Real-Life Petitions

It's while reading fiction that I'm most often internally moved to petitionary prayer, but it's during Mass that I'm most frequently exhorted to pray by someone else. The priest leads the congregation in prayer throughout the Mass, but there's a moment just before the beginning of the Liturgy of the Eucharist when we all pause to pray for specific intentions. A lector comes out to read a list of petitions from a binder, and we all meditate on them and reply, "Lord, hear our prayer." There are some regular, universal prayers (for the pope, for the sick) and some that are more topical (peace for people in a war zone, hope and healing after a natural disaster).

At some parishes, after the scheduled prayers have been read, the lector will say something like, "What else should we pray for?" and anyone can call out a prayer request from the pews. I've heard things like, "For my son, who is preparing for marriage, we pray to the Lord," or, "For all students preparing for exams, we pray to the Lord," or, "For a friend who is struggling with anxiety, we pray to the Lord."

I've always liked this moment in the Mass. At the parishes that hear Prayers of the Faithful from the faithful, I feel as though I'm participating in a census of the needs of the community. Not long after this time for spontaneous, public prayer, it's time for all the congregants to exchange the sign of peace as part of the Liturgy of the Eucharist. After hearing the prayers of others (and possibly contributing one of my own), I have the opportunity to offer help if I can, to pray with everyone else, and to simply know my fellow parishioners more deeply.

I'm not wishing an abstraction on my neighbors when I turn to them and say, "Peace be with you." The Prayers of the Faithful are a lesson in what Christ's peace will deliver us from: slavery to the fear of death, the misunderstandings and cruelties of others, our own habits of pride or contempt.

Not all parishes have people volunteer their prayer requests during the Mass but one can always ask for the prayers of a friend. After joining the Catholic blogging network at Patheos, I wound up in a Facebook group with the other Catholic writers on the site, and the reading recommendations and silly memes we share are frequently interspersed with prayer requests. Being invited to share our troubles and give prayer support makes the bonds of the community tighter (and some of the jokes funnier, since they're sometimes tailored to give comfort).

Hearing the prayer needs of others makes me more attentive to their lives as protagonists in their own stories. I've sometimes been surprised by the high levels of misfortune, sickness, and other problems that seem to afflict my fellow Patheos bloggers, but I think it's less likely that we're all unusually beset by "the slings and arrows of outrageous fortune" and more likely that I simply don't give other people as many opportunities to share their troubles with me. Without the possibility of asking me to pray for them, my secular friends are less likely to share with me their deepest troubles, not wanting to burden me with a problem I can do nothing about. In Catholic circles, technically no problem falls into this category.

Praying for others also helps me remember how expansive the lives of other people are, full of richness and pain, and much larger than the particular conflicts or joys that bring them into contact with me. The habit of petitionary prayer makes it a little easier for me to be patient in a fight or even to resist depersonalizing the people packed around me on the subway. If I pause to think about it, I realize that they would have many prayer requests to make if I knew them better, and that those requests would be particular to them as individuals. My ignorance of the full depth of their lives is not evidence that they are shallow.

When I go to friends to ask for prayers, I don't always feel comfortable inviting them into every part of my life, but I've sometimes found it helpful to ask someone to pray for me to repair a strained relationship, without naming the relationship. Asking for prayer help, at a level of intimacy that feels right, still allows my friend to know me better, to empathize with me, and to check up on me, reminded of my needs because of their inclusion in her regular prayers.

Solidarity through the Saints

Sometimes when I ask for prayers, my friend agrees to pray and also points me toward a saint who is somehow associated with my particular concern. Sharing my need or distress with that patron saint helps me connect with both the Church Militant (living Christians, still struggling to follow Christ) and the Church Triumphant (the saints, sharing in Christ's glory after death). Instead of isolating me through fear, pain, or shame, my troubles act as an introduction to people who love me, whose love is a reflection of the love that Christ offers me.

Just learning that there's a particular patron saint for my struggle does a lot to break the power of my unhappiness to isolate me. It means that my misfortune is not unique—not only is the saint herself at least one proof-of-concept person who faced the same hardship, but the fact that she became a patron saint for that struggle means that many more anonymous people found themselves in a similar situation. Enough of us are united by our need that someone was chosen specifically to watch over us. I can feel a sense of solidarity with all the people who have gone before me, mouthing the same prayer as I do: "Saint Zita, help me be kinder at work."

Saints also make for easy prayers. Some saints have particular prayers associated with them that I can use or adapt. Even if there's no script to follow, I can offer a prayer like the one above, where I just address the saint, name my problem, and leave the rest up to the expert.

However, there are times when I feel an impulse to pray (or a somewhat drier sense that prayer would be appropriate, without a corresponding urge to offer one) but don't have anything in mind to say. I don't want to develop a habit of waiting to pray until I have a well-crafted prayer to offer or know exactly what to ask. If my habitual response to the desire to pray is postponement, I'm afraid that, rather than coming up with a better idea of what to say in an hour or so, I'll just lower my sensitivity to the urge to pray. If I wait to offer prayers only in moments of peace and confidence, I'll lose the chance to invite God into all parts of my life, including the tumultuous moments when I need him most.

Praying the Bare, Honest Minimum

I've tried to work out some bare minimum prayers, prayers that I can nearly always offer honestly. That way, when I have the impulse to pray, it's easier for me to have a small way to close the circuit with God so that his grace can reach me instead of letting my self-consciousness short it out. After all, I'm no longer (most of the time) a Pelagian who believes I can work out my salvation through force of will alone, so it makes sense that I'll sometimes encounter problems beyond my power to handle on my own. I need some way of offering a small "Amen" to God, even if I haven't come up with anything particularly clever to add to it. I'm all right with assuming that if I manage that mustard seed of prayer, then God will handle the rest (or at least he'll enlighten me about the parts that are still mine to handle).

One of the hardest times for me to pray is when I'm in the middle of a fight, and I don't quite want everything to be patched up between me and the other party. I might be able to agree that it would be better in the abstract not to be angry forever, but in the moment, I'm too upset or hurt or proud to honestly desire peace.

I don't want to piously mouth prayers to God that I don't mean. If I habitually say things I don't mean in my petitions, those moments stop being acts of intimacy where I honestly lay my heart open before God. Lying sometimes, even if I try to categorize it as "aspirational lying" (saying the prayers I think I *should* want to offer), makes it feel more normal for me to be dishonest with God and myself.

Instead, I seek the smallest prayer I can offer honestly. Sometimes I turn the whole matter over to Mary and ask her to wrap me and my antagonist in her mantle. I ask her to take care of us in whatever way seems right to her. After all, Christ gave us all access to Mary as our mother when he looked down from the Cross and told her and John, "Woman, behold your son. . . . Behold your mother" (Jn 19:26–27). The very nice thing about mothers is that they have experience loving squabbling children.

I can trust Mary to behold me and the person I'm struggling with and to love us both. (This is not always something I can count on when I vent to a friend, who may try to "help" by finding *more* reasons to despise the person I'm in conflict with.) When we turn to Mary, we don't need to fear that we'll receive justice untempered by mercy, as we might from an earthly judge. A judge in a courtroom might decide to hang the defendant, but Mary will never reject her children or will their destruction. When we come to her to sort out our fight, she may honestly tell us that one or both of us are in the wrong, but she always desires that we both be restored to full life in Christ, not that one of us suffer to satisfy the retributive rage of the other.

I can offer my own petition to Mary or turn to the Memorare, which is short enough for me to memorize and even to say silently in the presence of others without seeming oddly withdrawn:

> Remember, O most gracious Virgin Mary, that never was it known that anyone who fled to thy protection, implored thy help, or sought thine intercession was left unaided.
>
> Inspired by this confidence, I fly unto thee, O Virgin of virgins, my mother; to thee do I come, before thee I stand, sinful and sorrowful.

> O Mother of the Word Incarnate, despise not my
> petitions, but in thy mercy hear and answer me.
>   Amen.

When I turn the matter over to Mary, I'm implicitly asking her to shelter my enemy as well as me, even if I'm too weak to ask for protection for my enemy explicitly. I can trust that Mary will make the prayer I was too worried or spiteful to offer, and thus I've found a way to minimally consent to that prayer. By putting myself under her protection, I've asked her to strengthen my heart, so that I can eventually echo her prayer with an undivided heart.

But sometimes, even that circuitous route to grace is too difficult to walk. Maybe I can't even honestly ask Mary to shelter me because I'm reluctant to accept her loving help, or am too mired in self-pity to feel worthy of her attentions, or because I'm so furious with my antagonist that I'd rather refuse help than receive healing alongside him. In those times, I have to find an even easier way to make a tottering approach to God.

When I can't honestly ask Mary to guide us both, I may be able to step back and say that I *would like* to be able to honestly ask Mary to guide us both, even if it's impossible for me to say at present. Well, if God grants that prayer, I will be able to return honestly and without reservations to implore Mary to guide us both, and then, when he grants *that* one, I can rely on Mary to undo the original knot.

Sometimes it takes several backward steps of "I want to want to want to . . . have Mary guide us both" before I can find an honest petition. Retracing my steps and lining up these dominoes of desire allows me to find a path, no matter how easy it needs to be, that lets me take *one* step toward Christ.

My prayer of last resort is shamelessly stolen from Shakespeare's *Twelfth Night*. Caught up in a heady whirl of cross-dressing, strained loyalties, and unrequited love, Viola, the protagonist, shakes her head and exclaims, "O time! thou must untangle this, not I; / It is too hard a knot for me to untie!"[2] I simply substitute "Lord" for "time."

Depending on the staging, Viola's lines can seem like a callous dismissal of her own role in weaving the tangled web or just a cry of pure confusion, but the Violas I like best are the ones who seem both well-intentioned and overwhelmed. She doesn't know where to start pulling on the knot, but she knows that the tangled hash of relationships around her is a disfigurement of some better plan. She knows it would be wrong for the status quo to rest undisturbed.

A knot is a wound in the world. Sometimes, when I don't know what to do or can't muster the strength to make things better, the best I can do is simply acknowledge that something is wrong, and that I want someone to heal me and it. So far, this is the prayer I can most reliably offer, even in my most prideful or stubborn moods, and I believe that the act of reaching out to God (even to hand the problem off) makes it easier for me to respond when he reaches back to me.

Chapter 2
Confession

When I entered the Catholic Church, my friends came with me to Mass to celebrate my Baptism, Confirmation, and First Communion. I had sent out the date in advance, and they dressed up for the occasion. Hugging me at the reception that followed, they recommended prayers that they loved and introduced me to saints who had supported them. But when I made my first confession a few weeks later, no one was with me except the priest; there was no expectation that this sacrament was the kind of thing I would announce or celebrate.

A Secret Sacrament

The Sacrament of Reconciliation is an oddly private grace. Priests and parishioners alike respect the seal of the confessional and refrain from discussing what is said during the administration of the sacrament. The priests are barred from repeating what they hear, and the laity are often discouraged from comparing notes after receiving the sacrament. (It wouldn't be very healthy to contrast the way priests assign penances for various sins in the same way that high schoolers sneak a look at each other's exam grades.)

Since this sacrament was so little discussed, I assumed that it must be a duty, not a joy, and my preparation was correspondingly dry. I readied myself for confession by reading through a set of prompts for an examination of conscience, learning the proper order of ritual phrases (helpfully tacked up inside most confessionals, in case I forgot), and checking parish websites to see when the sacrament was available. But all these logistical acts seemed a bit lifeless, nothing like the way people wrote and talked about other practices such as Communion or Adoration.

Confession has a tendency to fade into the background of Catholic life. My friends would bring up a hymn or a homily that touched them or talk about the consolation a certain prayer had brought them, but when they talked about confession, if it was mentioned at all, the tone tended to be generically thankful. Even if it were permissible to discuss what happens in the confessional in detail, I still wouldn't expect to hear much about it. The reason is simple: no other sacrament is premised on our screwups.

Even now, although I sometimes ask friends to confirm the start times of Mass or other parish events, I always check the parish websites myself for confession times, and if I'm heading out to make my confession, I rarely announce the fact as I do when I leave the house for Mass. It's hard to shake the feeling that, if I were to ask my friends when the priest was hearing confessions, they would be wondering, "What did she do that she needs to confess?"

Although my silence about confession was initially motivated by shame, the privacy still felt like something of a gift. As a religion blogger, I had made a somewhat public conversion. And though I knew I had no obligation to answer all the online questions about my spiritual life, I felt a little more defensive about deflecting questions in person. On the morning of my Baptism, my joy at joining the Church was mingled with a terror that, after the Mass, everyone was going to ask me what it was like to receive Christ in the Eucharist, and that I was going to wind up giving the wrong sort of answer. My friends were kinder and more tactful than I gave them credit for, but the anxiety made it hard to feel anything without becoming self-conscious. (Subsequent Masses were much lovelier.)

Confession posed no such perils. I couldn't imagine that anyone would ask me about my thoughts on *that* experience or that there would be anything I would feel comfortable sharing after the fact. The closest secular analogies I could think of were plea bargaining and parole boards, neither of which are appropriate cocktail party topics.

Soon after my conversion, once confession became something I *did* not just something I theorized about, I was surprised to find that it was my favorite sacrament. Confession reminds me of the orders of cloistered, contemplative nuns. Unlike their active sisters, they're seldom seen outside the cloister, and they can slip from our minds, but their lives of constant prayer support and inspire the religious brothers and sisters who come out to meet us in the world. Confession's quiet, secluded grace strengthens me to seek out all other graces.

Solace in "I'm Sorry"

Before I experienced sacramental grace of confession for myself, I had expected that the less frequently I *had* to go to confession the lighter and freer I would feel. I was partially right. There is a kind of lightness that comes with not having gone to confession in a while, but it isn't a feeling of freedom. It's more like the lightness of being unmoored or untethered: one is free insofar as one is not attached to anything, but that's a pretty precarious way to exist.

If I let a long time pass between visits to the confessional, putting off the sacrament until I commit a mortal sin, the venial sins I've committed become fuzzier and more indistinct in my memory and feel less consequential. However, that doesn't free me from their effects; the people I've slighted or scorned are still hurt, and the distance I've opened up between my conscience and my actions makes it harder for me to repent, learn, and make amends.

Or, to illustrate another way, the mother who is reading uninterrupted by her toddler might feel pleasantly free for a little while, but as the silence persists for longer and longer, it becomes more and more likely that the quiet indicates that something is wrong rather than that everything is conveniently tranquil. Going without confession means I'm not thinking actively about my guilt, but it gives me a wary feeling about the small sins I'm allowing to persist unchecked.

Catholics are obligated to go to confession only once a year, and only mortal sins require the sacrament before a Catholic can return to Communion, but I've developed a pattern of stopping by about once every three weeks. I wouldn't like the pressure of keeping track of my venial sins for a whole year and then unloading them on a priest all in one go. It's also not how I want to handle my relationship with God. After I've wronged a friend, I want to be able to apologize quickly, so that the suspense doesn't build up and make it harder to apologize at all.

Confession is my way of making up with God after damaging my relationship with him. Although it can be hard in the short term, I want to patch things up as soon as I can rather than leaving our relationship frayed and more vulnerable to new strains.

Confession strikes me as the most "small-*c*" catholic of all the sacraments, which is to say the most universal. Besides the Catholic Church, only the Orthodox and a few Protestant sects offer their worshipers confession with a priest, but the need for confession is recognized by everyone, Christian or not. We all acknowledge that we fall short of being the people we ought to be, even if we wouldn't all phrase it quite as Paul did when he asserted that "all have sinned and fall short of the glory of God" (Rom 3:23). Some people secularize the statement, saying we fall short of our duty or our potential, but either way it's clear we don't quite measure up and we know it. It would be nice to be able to apologize and make up for our lapses somehow.

If Catholicism isn't unique in diagnosing our weakness, it is unusual in offering us a treatment. The Catholic Church recognizes the universal malaise and fear that follows from our having transgressed and wounded God and our neighbors. Through confession, the Church offers us a way to receive God's mercy and healing. The hard part is preparing to accept such a generous gift.

The gift that Christ offers in confession is much larger than I could ever repay—and even wishing to repay him diminishes the magnitude of his mercy. If I were to try to total up the gift he bestows in just one reception of the sacrament, I would have to start my tally of the graces of

reconciliation and forgiveness long before I entered the confessional to seek absolution. Just knowing I will be going to
confession helps teach me what my sins are. Sometimes my
sins don't feel quite real until I'm listing them, either to the
priest or to myself in the line outside the confessional.

After all, a lot of my sins are inward ones (spite, contempt, impatience), which I might manage to hide from the
people they're directed at even as the unpleasant feelings fes-
ter within me. Some other sins are socially acceptable enough
not to draw comment (certain kinds of rudeness, passing up
opportunities to be kind, etc.), and they, too, can escape my
notice.

Until I pin down a sin specifically enough to be able to
describe it to someone else, it usually remains too vague to
convict me with more than a half-felt unease. There's a world
of difference between thinking, "I was a little more sarcastic than appropriate," and admitting, "At that debate, I kept
looking for opportunities for quips and pointed questions. I
kept treating my friend like a foil or a straight man, rather
than a person." Unless I get that specific, I don't feel enough
regret to want to amend my life. "I was too sarcastic" is
too dull and removed from the way in which it harmed my
relationship with God and others for me to feel urgent about
mending the fault.

Because preparation for confession is full of these epiph-
anies, my examination of conscience can feel like a process
of unpleasant revelations and loss. My brain, like everyone
else's, is good at learning patterns and intuiting causality, so it
doesn't take long before it decides that, because shame *follows*
preparation for confession, my examination of conscience is

what's *causing* those guilty feelings. If I find the process too upsetting or aversive, it becomes tempting to skip it since I have this unconscious sense that confession is *creating* those feelings of regret and that I'd feel like (or even *be*) a better person if I went to confession less often.

Defending Against Cognitive Bias in the Confessional

There's a close correspondence between a reluctance to go to confession and two cognitive biases: the *sunk-cost fallacy* and *loss aversion*. In economics, a sunk cost is something you've already lost that you can't recover later. If I buy the complete series of some television show on the recommendation of a friend, and the DVDs aren't eligible to be returned, their purchase price would be a sunk cost. No matter what I do with the DVDs now, I won't get my money back. The sunk-cost fallacy comes into play when we act as though we can magically avert or retroactively justify such costs.

Imagine that I realize after watching a few first-season episodes from my DVD set that I don't like the show very much. I might be tempted to finish the season, and even the entire box set, since I've already paid fifty dollars for the collection, and I don't want the money to go to waste. But whether I watch the remaining episodes or not, I am *already* out the fifty dollars. I have no duty to go on miserably binge-ing through the season just because I already spent money on the DVD set.

The fifty dollars is already lost—nothing I do will change that—but I could still avoid losing any more on the deal by putting the DVDs away and using my time for something that would actually make me happy. It does me no more good to try to delude myself into thinking I got at least fifty dollars of value out of the purchase than it does to eat "that which is not bread, and [spend] your labor for that which does not satisfy" (Is 55:2). Even so, we have a tendency to gorge on what makes us unhappy in order to avoid admitting we made a mistake in sampling it.

Admitting an error usually feels like a loss. Loss aversion tempts us to rationalize and delude ourselves in order to avoid the short-term pain of noticing a mistake or sunk cost, and it blinds us to what we can still salvage by backing away from error. This aversion comes into play for emotional losses as well as monetary ones and can be a serious obstacle to going to confession.

In order to avoid feeling the pain or shame of acknowledging my sins, I might rationalize that none of my recent transgressions have been mortal sins and that therefore there's no point in doing an examination of conscience and looking up the confession schedule. Or maybe I just keep telling myself I'm too busy to go to confession this week so I can put off an accounting of my faults until I have more time. Whatever the justification, I have allowed loss aversion to do its work and shield me from experiencing the short-term pain that comes with honest reflection at the long-term cost of not acknowledging my errors and going on hurting others without the chance to course-correct.

Happily, since I recognized this spiritual struggle as a specific flare-up of a bias I'd read about, I could turn to scientific literature to look for helpful countermeasures. Just knowing the name of the bias helps me recognize this pattern of thought and avoid rationalizing reflexively. When I get stuck in sunk-cost thinking, it helps to remind myself explicitly that the loss is already real, even if I'm only noticing it now. In the DVD example, I've *already* spent the money, a week or so before I know enough to regret the purchase. When I review the past week outside the confessional, I've *already* been unfair to my debating friend before I acknowledge it was wrong. The sin isn't being repeated or reinforced just because I'm finally thinking about it honestly.

It also helps me, as the queasy feeling of loss asserts itself, to remember that I do want to experience and acknowledge this feeling. My regret is a gift; it helps direct me away from sin and toward the healing promised in the sacraments, including the one I am about to receive. If I forget that, or have trouble believing it, I just imagine what the alternative would be like.

An insensitivity to any moral pain and disorder I leave in my wake would ultimately be just as destructive as congenital analgesia—a condition that leaves its sufferers unable to feel physical pain. Although I might envy that defect at the moment I accidentally slam a door on my hand, pain is a valuable source of information. People with analgesia have to vigilantly fill the sentry role that their nervous system has abdicated; otherwise, they could leave their hand on a hot stove, unaware they were being burned until their noses told them what their pain receptors could not.

As I am, my moral senses lie somewhere in between the responsiveness of my physical senses and those of a person with analgesia. I *sometimes* have a split-second reaction to sinning, but it's not as noisy as the reaction I have to spilling hot oil on myself at the stove. I can't rely on my moral reflexes alone to protect me from moral danger. I depend on more deliberate reflection to be able to notice the injuries I do to myself and others and to have the opportunity to treat them.

So when the confessional forces me to acknowledge the gravity of my sin by verbalizing it, I try to remain attentive to the feelings of loss and guilt that wash over me. My overprotective brain tempts me to hide from the ache or minimize it through rationalization, but I remind myself that I'm here to experience the pain in order to learn from it. Confession is the moment when I finally stop ignoring or muting the signals that God's grace has been sending me. It's the moment when I stop behaving like the little girl who falls down and gashes her knee but keeps her eyes screwed up shut so she doesn't have to see how serious the cut is. I can only seek healing for the wounds I've caused if I'm willing to look at them.

The Unfairness of Forgiveness

If it were enough for me to face my sin and regret it, there would be no need for the Sacrament of Reconciliation. But I have a tendency to forget this fact about confession when I'm actually in the confessional. I sometimes act as though the healing that occurs through the sacrament happens solely as a result of my labors of regret—as though I could have managed absolution independently through my trading prowess.

Usually, the hardest part of confession for me comes after I've listed my sins, when the priest assigns penance. I typically feel that the prayers he tasks me with are too light, that my confession hasn't been *fair*. And I'm right, sort of. The penance I'm given isn't fair—it's merciful. My Our Fathers or Hail Marys don't counterbalance the harm I've done to others, and they don't magically render me innocent. What they do is give me a way to cooperate with the grace that Christ is offering in restoring me to communion with him. My penance is more akin to the "Thank you so much" we offer in response to a gift than to the payment we offer to close out a debt. My desire for a "fair" exchange is as gauche and inappropriate as offering to pay your benefactor the difference between what they spent on your birthday gift and what you think they *should* have spent.

Confession isn't a trade in which I barter my regret for forgiveness. My repentance doesn't make me *deserve* this gift; it just means I've stopped hiding from Christ's mercy and started cooperating. When I consider the form my cooperation takes, I sometimes imagine myself as a radiologist imaging and treating a cancer.

When sin grows in me like cancer, I might be able to spot and excise a particularly painful growth, but the little threads that feed it are too subtle for me to identify and remove. For example, I might regret a wrathful word without realizing that I got so impatient and angry because I hold on to my time in a miserly way. Working on my own, I can only identify and treat individual metastases while leaving the roots intact and free to recolonize the spaces I've cleared.

When I go to confession, I remind myself that full healing does not and cannot depend on me alone. My job is not to mend but to allow the Holy Spirit to help me identify the problem and to submit myself to treatment. In a hospital, a radiologist traces out the shape and location of a tumor, models it as best she can, positions the beam of radiation, and then gets the heck out of the way of all that energy. In the same way, I have to hold still in order to avoid disrupting the delicate work of reconciliation.

Christ has the power to burn away sin, but he won't do it without my "Amen." When I name my sins, I try to keep my attention on them, without making excuses or trying to minimize them. I want them fully exposed to Christ, not shielded and secreted away from his ability to heal. Remaining honest about my faults for more than a fleeting moment is hard; my impulse is to flinch away from the pain, even if ignoring the wound opens me up to greater danger. I wish I could be anesthetized or restrained, so that I submit to treatment without the option to flinch away and disrupt the operation, but that would be shirking the only contribution I can make to the procedure.

Holding On to the Truth of Sin

When I'm struggling to be brave, I try to be like Janet, the protagonist from the folk ballad of "Tam Lin." In that story, the intrepid Janet falls in love with the knight Tam Lin, who is in the thrall of the Seelie Court of fairies. To rescue her lover, she has to pull him off his horse as the fairy procession passes and hold on to him, even as he shifts through a variety of dangerous forms. As Tam Lin turns into an asp and a dog and a bear and a burning coal, Janet's task is simply to hold on. She uses no magic in the story, but she is still a partner in freeing him from his curse. She cooperates as her strengths and faculties allow.

When I am trying to make a good confession, it feels as though my sin is going through similar shifts, trying to throw me off and distract me. While I try to keep it clearly in sight so that I can reject it, the fault changes forms and tries to pull me off course.

"But really, he deserved it. . . ."

"Come on, it was a perfectly normal reaction. . . ."

"Don't be so hard on yourself; you were tired or distracted. You weren't really responsible. . . ."

Each rationalization is a temptation to relax my grip and lie to myself about my error. If I refuse to see my fault accurately, whether by minimizing the gravity of the transgression or by downplaying my own complicity in the act, I'm making it harder for Christ to reach me and heal me. Imagine a radiologist who only imaged the left half of a tumor. She could expose the parts she mapped to the radiation, and they might shrivel and die, but the cancerous cells she neglected would be untouched and would quickly grow to fill the space left by their fellows.

Of course, all my analogies and good intentions aren't enough to guarantee that I've actually grasped the totality of my sin—or even the totality of the one incident I'm confessing—so that I can carry it to lay at the foot of the Cross. In order to cooperate with Christ, I pray for light, just the way I do during my review of the day in the examen. Since I can't see clearly enough to gather up my sin, I ask Christ to strengthen my sight and my hand, so that I can cooperate with him better in the future.

I ask him not to let me flinch away from what my strengthened sight shows me, even if I don't like what I see. Whatever sin I spot festering was already there before I looked; finally seeing it clearly is a gift, since it gives me the chance to reject it at last. And I'm not alone with what I see—Christ is gazing at my sin alongside me. Like Janet in her ballad, I've been told exactly what I must do, and I know the task before me will tax my strength, but not exhaust it.

Knowing God through Shadows

Being able to cooperate with grace and see my sin clearly helps me have a better knowledge and love of God. Seeing the ugliness of sin helps me to picture the beauty of God through *via negativa*—the negative way, or definition by denial.

A *via negativa* definition of God starts from something we know, even if that something is unlike God. Saying that God is infinite doesn't tell me much, since I've never experienced infinity. It's more honest (and helpful) to say that God is *not* finite, and thus position him outside the limits of my own experience. Through *via negativa* theology, even if I'm not sure what unalloyed goodness looks like, I do know that God does *not* share in the grotesquerie of my sins.

The confessional helps me understand my own nature with greater clarity as well. Before I prepare to confess, I'm a lot more likely to view some parts of my sin as a natural part of my self. But when I say something like, "I'm just a testy person," and speak about that fault as if it were part of my identity, I'm also implicitly attributing that sin to God's identity. If a tendency to sin were part of my spirit, rather than a malformation to be pruned away, it would necessarily have been shaped by God and have a share in his divine nature.

If I stop writing my sin into my soul, God turns out to be bigger and more beautiful than I let myself imagine. As I enumerate faults in confession, the freedom from sin that

Christ died to bring us becomes achingly specific. He died to free me from gossiping and contempt and anger. None of these is permanent; he made it possible to live without them.

It would be as strange to think of these faults as my natural inheritance as it would be to define a cancer as part of myself and refuse to be separated from it. I'm struck (more often inside the confessional than out in the world) by the absurdity of the excuse "Well, I'm only human." When I lay aside sins and ask for the grace to go forth and sin no more, I am being more human than ever, for the common vocation of all humans is sainthood.

Healed Is Not Unbroken

Confession aids us in this vocation to sainthood by transfiguring our sins through grace. When I arrive to confess, I am wounded. When I leave, I am healed, but I still may carry the marks of what I've done. And yet, that spiritual scar isn't a purely sad memento, a reminder only of where I was pierced by sorrow and anger. In that scar, I can also see where Christ touched me, brought the edges of the wound back into alignment, and held them until they healed.

The way Jesus mends me reminds me of a Japanese ceramics technique called *kintsugi*, in which valuable ceramics that are cracked or broken are fixed using a very unusual glue. The craftsman mixes gold dust with a special resin and uses this adhesive mixture to fill in the new cracks or to piece the entire pot back together. After the bond has set, the crack is still visible, but now it resembles a vein of pure gold. This is a kind of mending that draws attention to itself.

In confession, God mends the wound of my sin with his grace, and the resulting scar can be beautiful. The shining brand that remains is a gift—a reminder that I depend on God's mercy, and that his mercy is free for the asking. This kind of healing means that I can't think of my original sin in isolation from the forgiveness that was offered to me. The vein of Christ's love twines through my regret and penitence, keeping them from sliding into despair.

The next time I'm tempted by this particular sin, I can glance at my beautiful scar and remember that Christ intervened to help heal me of its rot. When I am confident in his power to save, I'm rarely tempted to presume upon that forgiveness. Instead, I feel more willing to pray for help and ask Christ or one of his saints to interpose himself between me and this temptation. Remembering how Christ was willing to heal me from this wound once encourages me to believe that he would want to help me avoid harming myself in the first place. The evidence of a previous intervention helps me avoid thinking of myself as too mired in error to be worth helping.

My experiences in the confessional remind me that fallen man is forgiven, not perfect. When I wind up on a prideful tear, I am like a pot spiderwebbed with cracks, achingly fragile, that refuses to submit to *kintsugi* because I don't want to mar my own false image of myself as whole and undamaged. If I feel that I bear relatively few marks of Christ's grace, it is probably not because I did not need the grace. It is more likely that I have neglected to seek it.

Scars, imperfections, and asymmetries cannot distance me from Christ. In his Incarnation, he inhabited and divinized this part of human life and suffering. When he rose from the dead, Christ still bore the stigmata and the other wounds he had endured on the Cross. Those marks testified to the torment he experienced, the reason he bore it (for our sake), and his power and authority to triumph over all miseries, including death.

In her essay "Grand Unified Theory of Female Pain," Leslie Jamison argues that there's something unique about a wound that sets it apart from all the other ways we have of categorizing pain and suffering:

> Different kinds of pain summon different terms of art: hurt, suffering, ache, trauma, angst, wounds, damage. . . . Wound implies *in media res*: The cause of injury is in the past but the healing isn't done; we are seeing this situation in the present tense of its immediate aftermath. . . . A wound marks the threshold between interior and exterior; it marks where a body has been penetrated. Wounds suggest that the skin has been opened—that privacy is violated in the making of the wound, a rift in the skin, and by the act of peering into it.[1]

Confession happens *in medias res*, while I am still touched by sin and struggling to find my way out of it. The forgiveness I receive is an act of intimacy granted by Christ, who left his wounds on his body so that we could reach him more easily, so that we had something to palpate and understand like the apostle Thomas, or a way to be joined to him as we ask in the Anima Christi: "Within thy wounds, hide me."

Christ must having been thinking of people like me, who like and are fed by signs and stories, when he left his death visible on his resurrected body. His stigmata are an outward sign of his unity with us, a symbol of the glory of the Resurrection, and a way of keeping my attention on the Cross.

Oriented toward God

As a sacrament, confession is an outward sign of an inward grace. The penitence that strikes me and marks me when I make my examination of conscience and receive mercy echoes the humiliation and pain that Christ bore on the Cross. The correspondence Christ offers us between his suffering and ours makes it easier for me to be brave and honest. I don't have to be able to approach the confessional without fear because I know that I can unite my anxiety with Christ's own reluctance when he prayed in Gethsemane, "Let this cup pass from me; nevertheless, not as I will, but as You will" (Mt 26:39, NKJV).

The pain I feel and even the misery of being "heartily sorry for having offended Thee" is transfigured through prayer and contemplation of Christ's passion. I am only able to offend God because I have a relationship with him. If it's there to be damaged, it is also there to be cherished if I make a different choice.

I can make the first steps back in the right direction by cooperating with God as he forgives me. After I offer my little "Amen" to Christ's work in my heart and walk out of the confessional, his grace is seeded throughout the wounds I walked in with, ready to be cultivated and bear fruit.

In the end, we are all called to be wholly united with God. Christ prays for this unity at the Last Supper: "As you, Father, are in me and I am in you, may they also be in us, so that the world may believe that you have sent me. The glory that you have given me I have given them, so that they may be one, as we are one, I in them and you in me, that they may become completely one" (Jn 17:21–23). *Theosis* is the process of preparing for this ultimate reconciliation, and the Sacrament of Reconciliation is one of the most potent graces we are offered along the way.

Until theosis is complete, we're all weak and jumbled up, like magnets that have been heated or dropped and whose component atoms have lost their north-south alignment. Just as an electric current can reorient a magnet, confession helps reorient me, correcting and strengthening my spiritual orientation so that I'm pulled back toward God. A simple surge of electrical current won't cause a magnet to sprout legs and wander back for another burst of polarization. But confession, unlike electricity, can form a feedback loop, where God leads us to return to the sacraments again and again.

The Sacrament of Reconciliation bears fruit on an individual and a societal level; the grace granted to other people can help strengthen me, just as a strong magnet can briefly turn even a paper clip into a small, weak magnet. Confession primes us for all other graces by restoring our orientation toward God, so that we can follow his call through prayer, works, and other acts of love.

Chapter 3
Examen

Until I read Father Timothy Gallagher's book *The Examen Prayer: Ignatian Wisdom for Our Lives Today*, I wasn't sure what differentiated the Jesuit examen from the normal examination of conscience I was supposed to do before I went to confession. I could see how the examen, as a daily (for Jesuits, twice daily) meditation, might provide a certain granularity that a biweekly or monthly preparation for confession would lack, but as far as I could tell at first glance, the two processes were essentially the same: review the period of time since your last reflection, notice all the bad things you've done, and feel proportionately regretful.

Technically, an examination of conscience comprises only one (maybe two) of the steps of a five-part examen. The first step of the examen is reviewing the past day, looking for moments of joy, and expressing gratitude to God. Next comes praying to God for light and clear vision, to aid in reflection and judgment. Only then does the examen get to the review of errors and sins that looks more like a standard examination of conscience. The fourth step is asking for forgiveness, and the final step is asking for guidance and help in doing better the next day.

But even if an examination of conscience was only one-fifth of the examen, I thought it must be the most important part because it seemed the most grave and difficult. I assumed that all the other steps existed mostly to help me "screw [my] courage to the sticking place"[1] and be able to take an honest look at my sins of that day without wallowing in despair or self-pity. Before I was going to worry about all these little helpful steps, I wanted to develop a better awareness of my sins, especially the ones I committed habitually, since at this point they took place without much conscious reflection on my part. Unless I cultivated attentiveness during the day, I didn't see how I could make an accurate examen in the evening.

Starting Small with a Saint and a Sign

One of the simplest, smallest examens I began to make was inspired by Saint Genevieve of Paris. (I've made a practice of picking a random saint each month using Jen Fulwiler's saint's name generator[2] and reaching out to that saint through reading and prayer. Saint Genevieve is one of the saints I've been dealt.) She is known especially for her devotion to the Eucharist and for leading the city of Paris in prayer to repel a Hun invasion.

During the month I dedicated to her, I would pray to Saint Genevieve while the priest was preparing and consecrating the host at Mass. I asked Saint Genevieve to tutor me in her love and reverence for Christ in this sacrament and to prepare my lips to receive his Body. Whenever I prayed this way, I usually had a sudden awareness of some recent word or deed of mine that made me, in Isaiah's words, "a man of unclean lips," jarringly out of step with both Saint Genevieve and the Savior she loved and served. Luckily, Isaiah's epithet is followed in scripture by a sign of hope: "Then one of the seraphs flew to me, holding a live coal that had been taken from the altar with a pair of tongs. The seraph touched my mouth with it and said: 'Now that this has touched your lips, your guilt has departed and your sin is blotted out.' Then I heard the voice of the Lord saying, 'Whom shall I send, and who will go for us?' And I said, 'Here am I; send me!'" (Is 6:5–8).

When I knelt at Mass anticipating the Eucharist, I was waiting like Isaiah to receive the burning love of Christ made flesh in order to heal me. I asked Saint Genevieve to help me to lay my sins at the foot of the Cross and to desire only Christ, not the faults that still enticed me.

I wasn't making a full examen or even a full examination of conscience, but thinking of Saint Genevieve helped me regularly ask two specific questions: "What have my lips spoken that they shouldn't? What have I held back that I should have shared?" Focusing on this narrow concern allowed me to reap some of the benefits of the full practice, as far as I knew.

The specificity of the prompt made it easier for me to come to Christ in prayer than when I tried to answer the vague "What have I done wrong?" Furthermore, praying at Mass gave me hope that, even if my prayers were fumbling and awkward, I was at least making them right in front of Christ—as close to grace as possible.

I preferred to try out the examen and other important prayers after Mass or during Adoration because, as a beginner at prayer, I didn't like relying on my own words and thoughts to invite God into my life. I knew intellectually that prayer was encouraged anywhere and that God would help me any time I asked honestly, but I didn't quite believe it in my heart, and I had a tendency to wind up in a spiral of self-consciousness when I tried praying on my own. Later, it was easier to ask for light and clarity wherever I was, but at the beginning, I needed to feel that doing my part in prayer was just showing up in the right place, rather than saying the right words.

It turned out that in desiring to examine my conscience directly in front of God, I was unconsciously mirroring part of the structure of the full examen. In the Ignatian practice, petitioners pray for light and clarity before they begin reviewing their day and their acts. The daily reflection isn't meant to be done alone, as preparation for facing God again, but in God's presence and in tandem with him.

Even when I was relying on as much help as I could get by choosing contexts for prayer, nervousness derailed another of my attempts at a beginner's examen. While reading Catholic blogs and Catholic books, I had seen a suggestion to cross myself whenever I noticed I was sinning or was about to succumb to a temptation. I liked the idea, since it both drew my attention to the fault and gave me a small way to arrest my slide into sin and turn my attention and love back to God. The writers I read suggested a few different ways to take up this practice. One person recommended tracing a cross on my forehead when I sinned in thought, on my lips for sins in words, and on my heart for sins in deeds. Another assigned sins against faith to the head, against hope to the lips, and against charity to the heart.

This kind of review and repentance sounded beginner-sized to me. As with my prayer to Saint Genevieve, the areas of evaluation were specific enough to keep me attentive; and because the prayer practice gave me something to do once I noticed an error, it directed me toward contrition rather than rationalization or moping.

Unfortunately, the public nature of the practice made it very hard for me to turn it into a habit. I suppose crossing myself in these small ways could technically be a tool for evangelism, but I don't like to explain to my friends that I've just made the Sign of the Cross over my heart because I was in the middle of thinking something fairly petty and unpleasant about them. So instead of running the desired "sin, notice, and repent" cycle, I was doing something more like "sin, notice, look around the room to see if I'm observed, try and decide whether to go for it, and get distracted by logistics." When I tried to maintain the practice only when I was alone, I lost the habit entirely.

The Full Examen

After my experiments with parts of the examen, it was time for me to approach the intimidating practice itself. My fumbling attempts at replicating it in miniature had made me wish to keep it up. I hoped that because the examen was widespread, whatever was hard for me was hard for at least one other person in approximately five hundred years—that meant there might be some advice that would help me. I picked up Father Gallagher's book again, resolving to try out all the steps he laid out.

First, I consider my blessings.

I had focused on tracking and categorizing sin, but in the actual examen, the assessment of my day doesn't come until the midpoint of the prayer, the third step. In its proper form, the examen does begin with a review of the day, but it is a review of my blessings, not my sins. These blessings might be unalloyed goods, such as a kind word from a friend or a peaceful lunch outside on a beautiful day, but they could also be good responses to trying circumstances, such as choosing to close a link to a gossipy, unpleasant website a second after clicking on it or putting aside anger and resentment when a project is delayed at work.

When I began my little examens by considering my sins, I was usually inward-focused, thinking only of myself and looking at myself in the same way that I would a buggy program or a jammed piece of machinery: what's wrong and how can I fix it? Beginning with gratitude forces me to consider to *whom* I am grateful. Suddenly, I'm not alone in my diagnostic troubleshooting—there's someone else peering under the hood with me, and God's gaze is a lot warmer and more loving than mine tends to be. He sees a person to be healed, while I think about problems to fix, by brute force if necessary. When I lose track of God's love, the litany of good things in my day makes his love more concrete and immediate.

Next, I ask God for light.

After counting my blessings has shifted my perspective a little, I then pray to refine it further, asking God for light and clarity to guide me in the rest of the examen. When I first tried praying the examen without the steps written out beside me, I kept reversing the first two steps and assuming that a prayer to see clearly must precede the consideration of gratitude. After all, wouldn't I be better off reviewing my blessings in the same light of clarity I'm requesting for reviewing my lapses?

The request for light in the second part of the examen is, in essence, the honest version of Benedick's exclamation in Shakespeare's *Much Ado About Nothing* regarding the power love has to transfigure our understanding of the world. Seeing his friend in love, Benedick wonders aloud, "May I be so converted and see with these eyes?"[3] In the second stage of the examen, I repeat his words, but leave off the question mark. I can sympathize with the stubborn Benedick, which is why I like borrowing his words. "Clarity" sounds safe and dull, a mere sharpening of the vision you already have, but Benedick understands that swapping out your perspective for someone else's, even if the new vantage point is better, is transformative and more than a little bit scary.

In order to want to look through someone else's eyes, I need to trust that person's vision. The first stage of the examen helps remind me of the reasons I have to place this trust in God. Even if my understanding of the blessings God gives is imperfect, reviewing what I *can* discern of them makes it easier for me to draw closer to God and to ask to see with his sight.

It's not that reviewing blessings automatically makes me feel happy or fortunate in my gifts—I might be praying the examen after an unusually trying day. That's why I like including moments of noticing and turning away from temptations as blessings, along with brighter pleasures. Placing the cruel word I swallowed in the category of "blessing" helps me keep the battle lines clear in my mind. God is too large for me to know completely; however, I know my own faults and temptations *very* intimately, and I know that God stands opposed to them. Even if I'm not swept away by the love of God every day, marking these kinds of blessings reminds me that he is my comrade in arms, there to help me face the next fusillade. You don't need to know everything about a comrade to be able to trust him in extremis.

With the light I'm given, I review my faults that day.

Once I've remembered the nature of my relationship with God through a review of my blessings and have relied on it by asking for light, it is finally time to review the day, noticing ways I fell short of who I should be. The defects in my day could include mortal sins but smaller blemishes also count. When I look over the day, I might reflect on the cutting way I shut someone up, my negligent indifference to a friend's need, or my delaying work on someone else's project because I felt spiteful that *my* project had been delayed. It doesn't matter if the sins are small in the sense that nobody got knocked down; sins of all sizes stem from the same error—a callousness toward others and a weakening of the love I should bear them.

Once my faults are clear in my mind, I ask God to forgive them.

The review step is immediately followed by the fourth stage of the examen: regret and asking God's forgiveness for the way I've hurt others and spited my own *telos*—my purpose and best self. Often, the third and fourth steps bleed into each other when I pray the examen because the simple act of reviewing my errors in the peace of an examen (rather than in the moment of committing them) enables me to recognize them as harsh, discordant notes and to honestly wish that I could find a way to bring them back to harmony. If a fault is more stubborn, I might just note it, along with my mixed feelings, and return to it in its proper place, once I finish the review of my day.

Finally, I anticipate how I will start over.
In the last stage of the examen, I look forward to the day that is to come, newly informed by my review of the day that just passed, and decide what I'll do tomorrow. Maybe I need to look up confession times and plan to receive that sacrament so that I may make a clean break with some of the sins I've grown attached to. Maybe I need to apologize to someone or, if I wronged someone in a one-off encounter, make some practical plans about how to hold my tongue for the sake of the next person who encounters me in that mood. Or maybe I want to be sure to repeat one of the good things I did today with a new appreciation for doing it in tandem with God, who helped me to see its goodness and rejoice in it.

Sharpening Discernment through Imitation

That was the theory, anyway, and I found it helpful for a month or two, but then I started to get stuck again. My examens frequently felt dry and repetitive. I would go over blessings, ask for light, and then reach the stage of review and think, "Well, it was a pretty ordinary, uneventful day. I got up (slightly late), went to my job, did my work (mostly), didn't have much cause to talk to my coworkers, then came home, ate dinner, did some writing, did some reading, futzed about on the Internet, and went to bed (slightly late)." There weren't any great sins or, as far as I could tell, any great virtues.

Each day's review started to resemble yesterday's to the point that I didn't feel I had anything new to learn from it. It became harder to muster enthusiasm to fully engage in all five steps, rather than just cursorily ask myself, "Did anything unusual happen today?"

The most I felt I was learning was that it probably wasn't such a good idea to go to bed a little too late and to linger in bed and be rushed in the morning, but this didn't seem like a pernicious case of sloth so much as ordinary disorganization, no more morally salient than my not making the bed every morning.

The examen is part of Saint Ignatius's Spiritual Exercises because it is supposed to strengthen one's capacity for discernment, the ability to sense God and cleave to him in the very great and very small matters of life. But I had stalled out and didn't know how to proceed deeper into the exercise.

I knew what I *wished* my examen did. I had been struck by a passage in *The Presence of God*, where Father Anselm Moynihan, O.P., describes the fruits of such iterative spiritual instruction—progressing from crudeness to sublimity:

> When a sculptor is making a statue, he has first to hack and hew the marble somewhat in order to get it into a general rough shape. But then, when the rough outlines are complete, he can use smaller tools and more delicate touches. Finally he will finish off the work with touches of an exquisite fineness. That is the way God deals with us. At first he shows himself only in the big events of our life; only the big blows seem to come directly from his hand. Then, when these have knocked us into some sort of shape—which they will do in the measure of our submission to his will—he

seems to touch the soul more frequently and more delicately. Finally, if we are true to these touches, God's hand will appear in everything that happens to us; nothing, even the most trivial, but will have an essential part in the fashioning of our soul.[4]

I wanted to cooperate with this process as much as I could, to be better shaped by God's delicate touches, but I couldn't improve my discernment by sheer desire or force of will. The best idea I could come up with was to broaden my experiences, so that God could correct my vision using more examples. It was as though I was grading every single day according to the same answer key; in order to keep learning, I wanted to give myself room to do *different* good things—or at least have the opportunity to commit and correct *other* mistakes. If my days all felt the same, I needed to work harder on shaking up my routine and finding inspirations for what to change.

I didn't know quite where to start. I found some help in the lives of the saints and in spiritual memoirs such as Augustine's *Confessions*, John Henry Newman's *Loss and Gain: The Story of a Convert*, C. S. Lewis's *The Screwtape Letters*, and Dorothy Day's *The Long Loneliness*. These books helped stoke my desire to be more virtuous and helped me realize that some of my faults were really vices, not just natural, unalterable limits on my patience, but I found it very hard to jump straight into imitating the lives of saints.

There was a gulf between me and the writers I was reading. Part of that gap was how much further they'd progressed in spiritual growth than I had, but part of it was just the difference in our circumstances. It was hard to figure out "What

Would Augustine Do?" because he had lived so long ago, in such different times. It was difficult to translate the virtues John Henry Newman expressed as a cardinal into equivalent virtues for a twenty-something policy researcher.

Instead, many of the most fruitful models I found were Catholic bloggers, especially mommy bloggers. When I opened up Jen Fulwiler or Calah Alexander's blog, I was able to read, instead of straight apologetics, stories of how their faith and prayer practices influenced their everyday actions. It was like being invited to listen in on someone else's examen; the writings of other bloggers helped me learn by example.

Even before I converted, I found these kinds of blogs helpful in forcing me to think about Catholicism as a living faith, not a field of academic study. After my conversion, their specific stories (finding ways to provide hospitality to a neighbor's kids, making choices about swearing, etc.) gave me a better lexicon of lived experience to compare my own life to.

Reading about the small choices made by others let me know them better, sometimes well enough to try to imitate them. The process was an adaptation of a clever idea my Catholic boyfriend had come up with in college when he was running for president of our debating group (the largest extracurricular on campus). Needing to reliably know all the members' names and faces, he did the logical thing: made flash cards, practiced every day, and aced it.

But once the election was over (he won), he still had the flash cards and no particular use for them. Inspiration struck: every week, he drew one person from his deck, left his or her picture out in his dorm room where he would be sure to see it, thought of a particular virtue of the person he had chosen, and tried to imitate that virtue for the week. Any given week, he might be trying to grow in intellectual curiosity like Dylan or merit trust like April or develop kind attentiveness like Alexander. Each week, he got the chance to reexamine his behavior through the lens of a particular, personalized virtue; he also tended to grow in love for the classmate he was imitating, since he was paying special attention to whatever was most beautiful about that person.

Instead of just reviewing the events of my own too-routine days, I began to single out a virtue of a specific friend or writer and revisit my examen considering how I could have imitated that person's curiosity about others or warmth while listening or willingness to trust others (specifically by being willing to delegate). Sometimes the disparities were subtle, but sometimes the differences leapt out at me.

Expanding the Examen Outward

In one of the example examens that Father Gallagher includes in his book, a woman realizes during her examen that she had missed a chance to be supportive to a coworker who was having difficult personal issues. Her story made me realize I had no idea whether I'd missed such a chance myself over the course of my day. As a rule, I didn't have deep enough conversations with my workmates to have the chance to be supportive. Here was one of the reasons my examens were so dry—when I was too careful with my investments of time or emotion, I was rarely at risk of being asked to be good to others.

Now, my examen started to feel more like a *Choose Your Own Adventure* book than a quiz or a checklist. My reviews turned up some moments of clear sin or clear grace, but I found many more times when I didn't seem to have the options to do good that other people had. I needed to take a look at what previous choices or structures in my life were obstructing the good I could do.

Sometimes, the fix was easy, or at least easy-ish. In one case, a friend I'd met through her Catholic blog was going through a very difficult personal struggle, and I felt too far away to offer anything but prayer. Prayer was *something*, but I still felt unsettled when I reviewed my day and made note of what seemed unresolved. Turning over in my head the possibility that I was selling prayer short didn't bring me the renewed sense of consolation Saint Ignatius often experienced when he went through a process of discernment.

No, I realized, I was selling *myself* short. I had been too quick to assume that I couldn't do anything but pray, just because I couldn't think of anything to do that was part of my usual repertoire of helping. After pondering what some of my friends might do, I had my marching orders and my consolation: I mixed up a batch of double-chocolate-chip-espresso cookies, got my blogger-friend's mailing address, and sent the cookies off the next day.

A failure to bake cookies would never have come up for me in my original model of examen. It might be an omission, but it's hardly a sin. The habit of an exploratory, outward-looking examen turned out not just to help me prune faults but also nurture virtues. Without its deliberate, broadened reflection, I'd have been much more likely to just ignore my discomfort with the way I was helping my friend since there was "nothing I could do."

I began praying the examen thinking of it as a solitary experience, a basic diagnostic and repair service for souls— the spiritual analogue of the "Please Wait, Updating . . ." message from my computer. I would never have thought of debugging as a social activity. However, once the examen rooted itself in my life, I realized I couldn't make a fruitful exploration of my day without relying on others.

First, I needed to ask God to let me see through his eyes; I needed a personal guide to augment my vision, not an inert instrument. And even after I received his light and clarity, it wasn't enough to just turn that vision inward. In order to sharpen my sight, I had to broaden it outward, and gazing at other people has turned out to provide the best learning experiences. What I imagined as a quiet retreat from my life to examine it from the outside has turned out to embed me further into my life and my relationships with others, as my soul is refined through imitation and service.

Chapter 4
Rosary

I started saying Hail Marys before I believed in God.

I was in the midst of dating (and arguing with) that nice Catholic boy, and I was trying to find a way to give prayer a fair chance without doing anything that felt hypocritical or dishonest. I didn't expect prayer to be useful, but I thought a little spate of it might constitute due diligence—putting my spiritual phone back on the hook, so to speak, so that God could call if he existed (and wanted to). Since I had no expectation of supernatural benefits from the experiment, I wanted to find some small petition of practical utility even to an atheist so that I wouldn't be entirely wasting my time.

The Rosary was the most Catholic thing I could think of, but saying the whole set of prayers would take much more time than I wanted to spend on the project. Hymns to God might sound lovely, but they felt too dishonest since I didn't believe in the entity being praised or petitioned. The Hail Mary was short enough to never feel inconvenient and turned out to fill a need.

Breaking Circuits with Mary

I have a bad habit when I am upset with someone or feel I've been wronged of indulging in uncharitable thoughts, luxuriating in magnifying the faults of the person who offended me.

If a schoolmate called me a bitch, I imagined her unleashing a longer, more creative stream of invective. If a coworker dismissed my idea, I pictured him actively subverting me.

Since I was something of a Stoic, these daydreams didn't make me angrier; they made me feel calm and strong. I could imagine the unkindness of others, cruelty much worse than what I currently faced, and decide I could withstand it. It was a point of pride that I wouldn't let these imagined offenses (or the real, milder ones) have any power over me. These reveries made it easier for me to keep my temper and appear to turn the other cheek, but what I was cultivating wasn't charity but callousness.

I realized a good long while after I was old enough to know better that I'd been inculcating a poisonous kind of indifference. When I pictured my enemy behaving badly, part of me wanted the fantasy to be real. I did want to know I was strong enough to endure unpleasantness, but more than that, I wanted to be wronged badly and unambiguously enough so as to have no further obligation to be kind to my tormentor. I wanted permission to walk away with no further duty to my antagonist. I didn't want the opportunity to be cruel in return—not usually—just the option of being indifferent, which I instinctively felt would be unjust in the absence of the transgressions I imagined.

By the time I understood that this spiteful habit needed to be throttled, I had practiced it for so long that it was a reflex upon believing myself to be wronged. The habit kept kicking in even after I realized it wasn't one I wanted to keep. What's worse, I'd spent more time reliving some of these spiteful imaginings than actually living with the people I was picturing, so my unkind mental images of these people were more vivid to me than their real selves.

Habits, physical or mental, are hard to break. Once a rut is worn in the mind, it's hard to keep one's thoughts from settling into the same old groove. Simply trying hard not to repeat the old pattern is rarely effective. Even if I silently repeated, "Don't think uncharitable thoughts!" as intensely as I could, I'd still be keeping the old reflex at the front of my mind. I had a better chance of derailing the old habit if I substituted a completely different action in response to the circumstances that triggered it (feeling wronged or upset).

And that's how Mary entered my life.

A Hail Mary seemed like a decent candidate for a mental circuit breaker that even an atheist like me could appreciate. If I recited the prayer in my head the moment I felt wronged by someone else, then for at least thirty seconds I *wasn't* fantasizing that my opponent was worse than he or she really was. By the time I got to the end of the prayer, the triggering circumstances might have passed and, with them, the impulse to indulge in uncharitable thoughts. If not, I could always recite the prayer again.

At the time, I picked the Hail Mary simply because it killed two birds (opening the connection to God in case he existed and derailing my bad habit) with one stone. But I could also recognize, based on what I knew about Catholicism, that Mary was an appropriate mediator to recruit in the midst of a fight. And since I truly wanted to break the habit, I felt that leaving the door open to intervention was the closest I could get to an honest petition to a hypothetical God.

The Rhythm of Ritual

After my conversion, I picked up the Hail Mary again as part of the larger prayer of the Rosary. But if the Hail Mary had previously recommended itself to me because of its brevity and simplicity, the Rosary had neither of these properties. It was the most Catholic kind of prayer I could think of—a physical rosary is accepted as visual shorthand to establish a character's Catholicism in movies or television. However, though I'd seen rosary beads everywhere, I still had no idea how to use them. Attempting the Rosary required a cheat sheet to help me remember the prayers I didn't know by heart and recall which mysteries were grouped together.

A Rosary comprises a set of five mysteries (events) from the lives of Christ and Mary. There are four established sets of five different mysteries each—the Joyful Mysteries, the Luminous Mysteries, the Sorrowful Mysteries, and the Glorious Mysteries. Each mystery is allotted ten Hail Marys and a couple of other short, rote prayers, during the reciting of which one is to meditate on the particular mystery assigned.

The only thing I'd absorbed about the Rosary was how to keep count by ticking off beads. I wasn't sure what the people I saw in movies and plays were thinking besides "One, two, three . . ." Previously, I had relied on a single Hail Mary as a distraction from an intrusive, uncharitable thought, but when I prayed ten Hail Marys in a row to cover a decade of the Rosary, I found myself distracted from the mystery I was supposed to be reflecting on.

As I meditated on the crucifixion of Christ, I couldn't imagine that any thoughts of my own could equal what I was contemplating. Even if I managed for a time to keep my mind on the mystery at hand, I was quickly diverted to self-conscious rumination about whether I was praying a *good* Rosary, which focused my thoughts on myself again, rather than on Christ and Mary.

As it turned out, ballroom dance practice techniques led me out of my little loop of "mystery misery." Instead of starting out trying to pray a good Rosary with the contemplative powers of a saint, I treated the repetition of the Rosary as though it were a foundation for later prayer, and all I had to do was practice keeping a steady beat.

In ballroom dance, the most exciting parts are the turns and sweeps, and some classes do teach you these fancy steps right at the beginning. Both leads and follows memorize their steps and then try to execute them independently and (if you're very lucky) in sync. As each dancer is trying to execute a memorized pattern, each relies on the music, rather than on their partner, to keep the steps continuous.

Good dance teachers spend a painfully long time on the "basic." The basic step for each type of dance is the underlying rhythm and technique for the more advanced steps, one that stays pretty much the same no matter what fancy move you're doing. My teacher told me to practice basic steps *everywhere*, so I spent a summer marching in place on the subway platform, or wherever I found myself, to the beat of "one-two *cha-cha-cha*" or "one-two-three *hold*, five-six-seven *hold*." The goal was to be able to slip into any of those rhythms as easily as I could my normal gait.

If I am following a dance partner with a decent lead, maintaining the basic is my *only* responsibility. As long as I keep my feet moving in the proper sequence and stay responsive to my partner, I can move through combinations I haven't learned, steered by my partner into the right place while my feet keep the right time. In fact, as my basic improved, it was sometimes easier to dance sequences I *hadn't* learned than to dance the ones that had been broken down and taught to me piece by piece. When I didn't know what I was doing, I could keep my focus on the basic. When I had a clue, I often tried to anticipate the next move and wound up botching it.

I tried to approach the Rosary with the same spirit I'd brought to my summer of basics. When I picked up my rosary, it wasn't to rehearse a solo, something depending solely on my own efforts. I was supposed to be God's partner, and he was to be the lead. I gave myself permission to focus only on *my* part—keeping up the basic structure of the prayer, without trying to anticipate any showy moments.

The Rosary turned out to be just as portable as my dance steps. I could practice it at bus stops with or without a physical set of beads, strengthening my habits and preparing to be swept into the dance by my capable partner. The Rosary lets me practice cooperation with God who, like my dance partner, asks for only one small, disciplined act on my end.

Picking up the beads and following the structure of the prayer puts me in the presence of Mary and Christ. And really, that is the extent of my responsibility when I'm praying. It's not for me to compel their intercession or force myself to achieve an insight into their lives. I just have to keep the rhythm so that I can follow without stumbling if anyone takes my hand.

Beginning to pray the Rosary in this way helped me stop avoiding a prayer I was afraid I couldn't live up to, but I was still a bit of a wallflower when it came to exploring the assigned mysteries. For a long while, the only version of the Rosary I prayed was the set of Sorrowful Mysteries.

The Sorrowful Mysteries—Standing among Christ's Persecutors

Catholics are supposed to either fast from meat on Fridays or take on another discipline; since I was a vegetarian already, I picked a Rosary as my Friday devotion. Each day of the week has a particular set of mysteries associated with it, and Friday, given its kinship to Good Friday, is matched to the Sorrowful Mysteries, so those were the ones I meditated on every week. Praying only the Sorrowful Mysteries gave a slight sense of imbalance to my relationship with the Rosary. My prayer life was like that frozen land of Narnia first discovered by the Pevensie children in *The Lion, the Witch and the Wardrobe*: "Always winter and never Christmas."[1] But that was the least of my worries.

I had trouble approaching any of the Sorrowful Mysteries without feeling intrusive or self-conscious. I had practiced the basic, but I still didn't understand what was supposed to come next. These five mysteries (the Agony in the Garden, the Scourging at the Pillar, the Crowning with Thorns, the Carrying of the Cross, and the Crucifixion itself) seemed too miserable and momentous to look at directly. So I didn't.

I tried to find something within each mystery that I *could* think about. Instead of thinking about the person at the heart of the story, I focused on people at the periphery. I imagined the person who made the crown of thorns and the effort that anonymous person might have put into coiling it. The soldier wielding the lash can inflict pain without feeling it himself, but the person binding together thorns must feel the same pain he is preparing for another. Was it possible to weave those branches together, pricking your own fingers, without feeling an ounce of sympathy for the person whose head you were going to wound?

It seemed unimaginable until I thought a little more about some private sins of my own and how I could turn pain into pride. Enduring pain in order to hurt someone else didn't always trigger sympathy in me. Sometimes it made me feel self-sacrificing and righteous; being willing to suffer myself in order to have vengeance made me feel nobler even though my sacrifice achieved nothing particularly good.

Sometimes I impressed myself with the level of effort I was putting into my pain-inflicting actions—as if the person preparing the thorns for Christ had spent time carefully braiding them, so that they would appear tidy and artful. Once I'm mired in a sinful, spiteful project, it's harder to admit I was wrong since I've put honest effort into my evil purpose; and it's almost as hard to admit I've wasted my time as it is to concede that I've spent it pursuing something ugly.

Wherever I looked in the Sorrowful Mysteries, I could learn a little bit about Christian action, even if I shied away from focusing my meditations on Christ himself. When I contemplated Christ's long procession to Golgotha, I meditated not on Christ himself holding up the Cross, but on the people lining his path. They taunted Christ as he passed for stumbling or for bleeding, for bearing the weaknesses of the mortality he'd taken on. I wondered what would have convinced them that they were actually in the presence of God.

It was hard to believe that strength alone would have convinced them, since ordinary humans can sometimes show great endurance. In their place, I might have expected God to reveal himself in his wrath. After all, the crowd had certainly treated him unjustly, so wouldn't I be able to recognize God by his divine authority and ability to punish? But a wrathful God would be just a scaled-up version of us—more powerful but no more kind or merciful. If I had been part of the crowd, I might or might not have been one of the people spitting or cursing, but I still would have been wounding Christ twice over—first by expecting nothing more of him than power, and second by modeling my idea of God on my low opinion of people (including myself).

The Sorrowful Mysteries helped me see how pain and anger distort our vision of God and the Good, but I needed the help of other, more peaceful mysteries to correct my vision.

The Joyful Mysteries—The Spreading Story of Salvation

The Rosary is a storytelling prayer. It moves along the arc of Jesus and Mary's experience and offers many points of access into their lives. Once I've been caught up in any part of the story, the narrative draws me "further up and further in!" as C. S. Lewis might put it.[2]

Even restricting my gaze to the humblest and most wicked parts of the Sorrowful Mysteries led me back, circuitously, to contemplate the nature of God. Finding my way into the Joyful Mysteries, I again felt I had to restrict my vision so that I had something smaller than God to look at while my eyes adjusted. I started moving through the Joyful Mysteries by directing my attention, not to Christ himself, nor even to Mary, but to whoever was speaking to Mary.

In the first mystery, the Annunciation, the speaker is obvious. The beginning of the Hail Mary itself is taken from the angel Gabriel's greeting to Mary when he reveals that she has been chosen to bear the Christ, if she consents.

Next, Mary's cousin Elizabeth greets her with "Hail, Mary," when Mary comes to her in the mystery of the Visitation and Elizabeth comes to understand the special role her cousin has taken on. Elizabeth is the one to exclaim, "Blessed art thou among women, and blessed is the fruit of thy womb" (Lk 1:42, KJV).

Joseph is the next to take up Elizabeth's refrain when, during the mystery of the Nativity, he might address his wife during her labor, murmuring assurances of her "blessedness," which he was just coming to understand himself—again, through the ministration of an angel in a dream (see Mt 1:20).

The last two joyful mysteries touch upon the time in the life of Christ about which we know the least: the years before he began his public ministry. When Joseph and Mary travel to Jerusalem for the Presentation, they are greeted at the Temple by the holy man Simeon and the prophetess Anna, both of whom could welcome the Holy Family with the sentiments expressed in the Hail Mary. And finally, when the child Jesus slips away from his family to preach in Jerusalem, his words blossom in the hearts of his hearers, who now can recognize the Holy Family when they come to retrieve their son in the fifth mystery, the Finding in the Temple.

As the words pass from one set of lips to the next, the sphere of God's grace grows. First, he speaks to a single individual, Mary. But his love is too great to be contained by one woman. It spills over to her flesh-and-blood family through her mere presence when she goes to visit Elizabeth. Next, Joseph is swept up into this great love, since by the bonds of matrimony he too has become Mary's family. When the newly sealed family travels to Jerusalem, God's grace expands outward from a single family to an entire nation. They are presenting Jesus at the Temple in obedience to Jewish law, and when the Temple accepts and blesses him, the people it serves receive a much greater blessing in exchange. Finally, as Christ begins to preach, the love he offers slips all bonds and lies before the whole world, freely available to anyone who will stop and listen.

Praying through the Joyful Mysteries and their story of expanding love reminds me a little of the documentary film *Powers of 10* by Charles and Ray Eames. These two filmmakers took their audience on a tour of the natural world, starting from the scale at which we live our lives, and then zooming out and in by powers of ten, until they had shown their viewers the vastness of the entire universe, which contains our solar system, which contains Earth, which contains us; and the infinitesimal tininess of the quarks that make up protons that make up atoms that make up molecules that make up us. The film allows us to wrap our minds around the very large and the very small because the Eameses make sure to start us off with a reference point our own size, a one-square-meter shot of a man and a woman picnicking.

We can compare everything else in the movie to that image to gain a sense of scale.

In a similar way, the different kinds of love stories contained in the Joyful Mysteries are easier for me to interpret in relation to each other. Each time I pick up the beads, a different story's scale may feel me-sized, but whichever one catches my attention teaches me how to look at the others. Some days, I feel connected to God at the one-to-one level Mary knew with Gabriel; more often, though, I sit much farther back, somewhere on the outskirts of the crowd listening to Christ at the Temple. If I can recognize love in any of these relationships and want to offer love in return, it's easier for me to recognize how the other scales of love and joy are present in my life. In a moment when I'm swept up in the love I experience within my church (at the scale of the Presentation), I can pray to offer that kind of love to my brother or my parents (at the scale of the Visitation). And if I am struggling to love at the scale of the Nativity (the people we adopt into our families), I can bring my confusion to God through Mary when I reach that mystery.

The Joyful Mysteries act like a benevolent riptide, making it harder for me to treat each kind of love I offer or experience as separate. No matter which inlet of love I find inviting to wade in, the current is waiting to bear me out to where all the waters are intermingled—as long as I am willing to immerse myself in the love that is presented to me. The Joyful Mysteries, which begin with Mary's great "Amen," invite me to make a small one, at any scale, to receive the chance to better know the God who is Love at all scales.

The Glorious Mysteries—Looking Where Christ Led

The Glorious Mysteries came to exercise a similar narrative pull on me. Instead of showing love at every scale, these mysteries introduce divinity and are appropriately expansive as a result. Compared to the Sorrowful Mysteries, which span a short period before Christ's death and take place entirely on Earth, the Glorious Mysteries felt overstuffed to me. I started thinking (privately) of the Glorious Mysteries as the "Wizard of Oz" mysteries, since in these stories "people come and go so quickly here!"[3]

The Glorious Mysteries begin with the Resurrection, when Christ returns to our mortal world having defeated death. But the disciples have only a little time to rejoice that he has been restored to them before he passes beyond their sight in the Ascension. Perhaps they would have mourned, but shortly after Christ leaves them, the Holy Spirit descends at Pentecost, sustaining them and preparing them to preach. Then the story skips much further ahead in time, to the moment when Mary, mother to the infant Church, passes out of the world and is taken up body and soul to heaven in the mystery of the Assumption. In the final mystery, Mary is welcomed into heaven and her Son crowns her Queen of Heaven and Earth (the Coronation).

The scope of these mysteries gave me spiritual whiplash. I had skirted the anguish of the Sorrowful Mysteries by restricting my gaze to the means of Christ's torment rather than the experience itself. I approached the Joyful Mysteries by relating the scale of each act of love to the others, so I could understand them by contrasts, even if I didn't fully comprehend any of the mysteries. But moving from Christ's resurrection to the arrival of the third person of the Trinity in the space of thirty Hail Marys was just too much.

However, as I prayed these mysteries over a period of months, their frenetic pace of revelation acted as a strangely helpful bait and switch. The sheer impossibility of contemplating the first few mysteries in this sequence made the Glorious Mysteries an attractive Rosary to pray when I was stressed or confused since I felt there had to be at least *some* kinship between my struggles and those of the apostles. When my jittery emotions lead me into contemplation of the relationship between divinity and humanity, the succession of these mysteries draws me onward, out of anxiety into the only peace that can answer my restlessness.

To approach the Glorious Mysteries, I imagined where Mary and the apostles were looking as each of these events played out in their lives. The very first mystery in the sequence, the Resurrection, happens out of sight of all mortal eyes. The disciples discover the risen Jesus by the tomb, but his resurrection had already been accomplished out of their sight. Christ had already defeated death and freed us all from slavery to the fear of death by his passion. The revelation of this work and everything that follows aren't necessary to save us but to give us joy and hope in the knowledge of God's work. Christ appears to the disciples after his resurrection to teach us who he is and how to follow him.

But the disciples, having seen their resurrected Lord, lose him quickly when at the end of forty days on Earth he rises to rejoin his Father in heaven. The disciples must strain as they look up, trying to hold him in their sight as long as they can, just as they all—particularly Peter—tried earlier to hold him upon Earth by urging him to avoid danger and death. Craning their necks, the disciples are oddly prepared for the next mystery, for they are looking up at the place from which the Holy Spirit will descend.

Yet at Pentecost the disciples have nowhere obvious to look when they are touched by the Holy Spirit. It isn't the corporeal kind of blessing they received from the incarnate, very visible Christ. I decided they have to be looking out across the crowds they find themselves preaching to in languages they do not know. As Christ tells them, "The eye is the lamp of the body. So, if your eye is healthy, your whole body will be full of light" (Mt 6:22). They received Christ in the flesh so that they could be blinded by the light of the Holy Spirit. They were emptied out in order to make space for the third person of the Trinity to enter into them, but instead of simply containing the Holy Spirit, the disciples let the graces they received spill forth from their eyes and lips to enlighten others. Although God has passed out of their direct vision, they keep him in view by serving others.

Mary, conceived without sin, never loses sight of God her entire life. So when she dies, she steps lightly out of this world and into the next—the Assumption. The way I imagined this singular mystery, Mary was so full of light from looking at God and bearing him within her that her whole body was suffused by glory, and the mortality that entered the world with sin had no further claim on her. She was already purified of everything we must discard through the struggles of death and purgatory. After all, heaven is unity with God, which she was living even in her earthly life.

The final mystery invited me to look along the path she trod to its ultimate end: her coronation as Queen of Heaven. I look at Mary, along with all the angels and saints in heaven, but she must still be looking at Christ. Before a crown can be worn, it has to be offered, and only Christ the King has the authority to crown Mary. When I think of Mary receiving her crown, I am reminded to despise all the prizes I can grasp and to desire only the gifts that God in his authority chooses to bestow.

The Glorious Mysteries help quiet, or at least redirect, my nervous energy by aligning me with the chaotic calling of the disciples. It is no sin to hunger for God or to pursue him with more zeal than wit, but I don't need to strain as though I'm being asked to *overtake* God or to anticipate his next appearance. That was beyond the ability of the apostles, let alone me.

If I simply try to keep my eyes on him, wherever he is present in my life, I am imitating Mary in my own small way and relying on God, rather than my own intelligence and energy, to let me know where to find him next. Ultimately, when Mary and the disciples kept God in view, he offered them more and more of himself, and they were transfigured in order to receive and share him. I try to follow their example.

When I don't know where to look for God, I can seek him out corporeally in the Eucharist, just as the disciples walked with him bodily after his resurrection. When it feels as though he has drawn away, I can remember where he went when he ascended. Fortified by that thought, I can remind myself that just as he ascended, the Holy Spirit *descended* and is with me particularly when I go out into the world to offer service. I want to remain in God's presence, to become so attentive to his gaze and direction that, when I die, I can look along Mary's path to the place where he waits and know him well enough to ask to be completely united to him.

The Glorious Mysteries tell the same truth that my patron saint Augustine recorded in his *Confessions*: "You have formed us for Yourself, and our hearts are restless till they find rest in You."[4] The Resurrection draws us after Christ, half exhilarated, half afraid, and the mysteries that follow teach us how to keep him in view. Hunger for God, even a frustrated hunger, is the beginning of the story that teaches us whom to seek in order to be sated.

The Luminous Mysteries—Tutoring in Transfiguration

I came to the Luminous Mysteries last since they were the newest set to be offered. Saint John Paul II introduced this set of mysteries in 2002 in an apostolic letter entitled *Rosarium Virginis Mariae*. The mysteries I had already familiarized myself with covered the birth and initial recognition of Christ, the suffering and death of Christ, and the resurrection of Christ and our preparation to follow him.

The Luminous Mysteries are chosen from Jesus' earthly ministry—his interactions with his disciples and the curious crowds that followed them. They cover his Baptism at the hands of John the Baptist, the Wedding at Cana, the Sermon on the Mount (the Proclamation of the Kingdom of God), the Transfiguration, and the Institution of the Eucharist at the Last Supper.

As I became acquainted with these mysteries, I started to think of them as the Matthew 5:17 mysteries, since they all seemed to fit within the scope of the promise Christ made: "Do not think that I have come to abolish the law or the prophets; I have come not to abolish but to fulfill." When Christ walks among ordinary people in their everyday lives, he exalts their rituals and practices. Just as he is transfigured and illuminated in the fourth mystery in this Rosary sequence, so does he transform the activities he participates in, bringing them closer to perfection.

Three of the Luminous Mysteries invite meditation on moments when Christ introduced his nascent Church to a sacrament. When Christ submits to Baptism, he divinizes the waters so that we can receive Baptism ourselves in holy water and become sealed to him. When Christ visits the wedding at Cana, he elevates marriage from a simple agreement or contract to a sacrament as he changes ordinary water into the richest wine. Finally, at the Last Supper, Christ transforms the Passover ritual from a reenactment of the sacrifice of a lamb to a new, living sacrifice of God himself. Just as the Jews offered and consumed their sacrifice in remembrance of God's historic mercy in saving them from earthly slavery to Pharaoh, so do Christians receive the Eucharist as God's mercy in saving us from our spiritual slavery to sin and the fear of death.

Throughout the Luminous Mysteries, I saw this pattern of transfiguration, moments when God let his divinity illuminate and exalt some part of human tradition until it was so holy that it was almost hard to understand. I had to pause and rest my intellect just as the disciples had to shield their eyes from Christ's light during the Transfiguration.

At first glance, the remaining mystery seemed not to fit into this pattern. When Christ proclaims the kingdom of God in the Sermon on the Mount, he institutes no sacrament. However, he does put the moral law through a kind of expansion. He tells the crowd, "You have heard that it was said to those of ancient times, 'You shall not murder'; and 'whoever murders shall be liable to judgment.' But I say to you that if you are angry with a brother or sister, you will be liable to judgment" (Mt 5:21–22); and, "You have heard that it was said, 'You shall not commit adultery.' But I say to you that everyone who looks at a woman with lust has already committed adultery with her in his heart" (Mt 5:27–28).

Christ is divinizing the old prohibitions and strictures by enlarging them. Instead of simply asking us not to murder, the bare minimum that could be expected of a thinking, loving being, he now calls us not even to hold on to anger, because that choice is also a kind of violence, to ourselves as well as to our brother.

As someone fascinated by abstract questions of moral philosophy, at first I thought that this mystery was about Christ transforming the *rulebook*, giving us a new, more exalted set of rules to follow. But I was so focused on the sermon and its speaker that I ignored its audience. The Sermon on the Mount isn't an act of editing the rules, I realized, but a public call to repentance. Christ isn't interested simply in tidying up the law; he wants to transfigure his hearers from pharisaical rule followers into saints.

While scrupulous people like me like to know the rules so that we can keep up with them, saints *know* they fall short of their duties and ask for help and mercy. When God answers their prayers, they spill over with grace and light, filled by something more potent than they could have thought to ask for. They are the great stone reservoirs, which, previously filled with water, now brim with potent wine.

This story of transfiguration through grace plays out over and over again during Christ's ministry, but I am particularly attached to the moments when he preaches the coming of the kingdom of God to large crowds. The sheer size of the throng is anonymizing, which makes it easier to imagine myself there, and to slip in among the listeners in need of transformation. It feels more natural to join the crowd than to project myself into the parables or the personal encounters of Christ with the people who followed him. Some of those stories are too far from my circumstances to seize me (the hemorrhaging woman in Matthew 9:20–22) or much too relevant for me to meditate on without shame (the rich man who would not sell all he had in Matthew 19:16–22). By meditating on the crowd, I can sneak up on learning how I need to be transfigured without frightening myself off prematurely.

The entire Rosary gives me the chance to join a crowd of witnesses asking to be changed. Whichever mysteries I settle down with, the stories offer me chance after chance to be drawn in to the life of Christ and Mary and to follow them. Even a partial Rosary, a few decades prayed before bed or during a walk, puts me in sync with many of the saints and the members of the living Church Militant. If I want to follow the vocation of a saint, I can't anticipate all the steps myself.

When I pick up the rosary, I am being tutored by the lives of Christ and Mary; but more importantly, I can just rest, dwell in peace, and allow them to offer me the kind of help I don't yet know enough to ask for.

Chapter 5
Divine Office

The prayers prescribed in the Divine Office (also known as the Liturgy of the Hours) were the first I offered after deciding that I did believe in God, after all.

I had come back to college for an alumni debate, and I'd been up for several hours arguing theological matters with a friend. Although I had enjoyed the afternoon's speeches on education policy, I still had burning questions about the problem of God, so after the festivities were over I pigeonholed an undergraduate friend, a Lutheran who was considering becoming a minister, to continue the discussion.

It was in his dorm room, on the night before Palm Sunday, that I finally changed my mind. But I didn't jump straight to the alleluias. First, I spent a while playing devil's advocate against my newfound faith, trying to make sure it would hold. After hours (following months) of debate, I wanted to keep probing and questioning for just a little while longer. But once I'd run through a number of objections and was finally ready to relax and just experience my new beliefs, I turned to my friend and asked him what we should do now. He said with delight, "Let's pray the Liturgy of the Hours!" and pulled out the breviary he kept in his room.

It was about two in the morning, a little late for Night Prayer and still early for Morning Prayer, but we knelt together to say the lines that open each of the seven Hours: "God, come to my assistance. Lord, make haste to help me." We alternated verses as we spoke the psalms, just as monks and nuns do in their choirs, until we reached the final "Amen."

When I woke up the next morning, at the opening of Holy Week, I found the readings for the Divine Office online, and I've been praying the Liturgy of the Hours ever since. (At least, I've been *intending* to pray the major Hours, with variable success).

Prayer as the Warp and Weft of the Day

The Liturgy of the Hours, which predates many of the splits and schisms in the Body of Christ, is a cycle of psalms and prayers that is most often prayed by the clergy and vowed religious but is available to the laity as well. Together with the Mass, it constitutes the public prayer life of the Catholic Church, and its roots stretch back past Christ's birth to the Judaism he was born into.

In Jewish practice, certain prayers are recited throughout the day, blessing and thanking God upon rising, eating, and going to bed. Early Christians carried over these devotions, using the psalms to speak to God and adding text from the New Testament as it was written and recognized. Over time, the structure of the breviary was formalized, and now the specific psalms and hymns for every hour of every day are available online as well as in print.

The basic structure of one of the minor Hours is reasonably representative of all the others. The daytime prayers have an opening address to God, a hymn, three short psalms, an excerpt from scripture, a concluding prayer, and a final expression of thanks to God. Praying all the Hours consistently will eventually lead you through all the psalms, just as attending Mass daily will let you hear the bulk of the New Testament.

As I prayed the Divine Office, I often felt that my day-to-day life was being bound together and put in order like the prayers in my breviary. If God reconciles all things and persons into one in him, the prayers of the Divine Office seemed to help my life conform to that plan. These repeated prayers, spaced throughout the day, repeated over the weeks, have served as the warp and weft of my worldly and spiritual life. They bind me closer to the people around me and lift me closer to God.

These simple prayers come across to me as a great, lovely, and complicated knot, like those created by the ancient Chinese knotting art called *Zhōng Guó Jié*. These knots are built up by many small crossings and loops, each step relatively simple, until the whole thing is pulled tight into a mass so lovely and so intricate that the observer can neither see how to unravel it nor desire that it be undone.

Freedom through Limitation

Yet despite my appreciation for this devotion and the simplicity of the prayers, I've struggled to make the Liturgy of the Hours a regular part of my life. At best, I've managed to incorporate these prayers into three-week segments of my life at a time, and then abandoned them.

One aspect of the Divine Office that has worked for me is the time-based structure of the prayers, which gives me built-in deadlines. When I tried to say a Rosary every day,

I had to decide every day *when* to say it. Since the timing was negotiable, I tended to put it off until it was bedtime and clearly too late to start. But the very names of the prayers of the Divine Office set limits on me.

If it was past noon, I couldn't very well make a case for saying Morning Prayer any longer. Times to say Morning Prayer were scarcer than times to say the Rosary, and this sense of impending loss lent a greater urgency to my decision whether to pray at eight in the morning. If I didn't say Morning Prayer *now*, I wouldn't get another chance.

Trying to integrate the Liturgy of the Hours into my life revealed more about my schedule than I'd ever gleaned from my calendar app. I kept trying to pray Night Prayer, but it was vulnerable to the same problems that had plagued my Rosaries. Morning Prayer had to be said before work, if it was to be said at all, but I had no firm limits on my evenings the way I did on my mornings. I just kept intending to say the prayer "before bed." If I tried to constrain the space of possible prayer time a little, by assuming it should be dark outside before I attempted Night Prayer, I still had a lot of possible slots between eight o'clock and (depending on the night) one thirty in the morning.

Aesthetically, I really liked the idea of making Night Prayer the last words I said before sleeping, but that goal was completely incompatible with my usual strategy for deciding when to turn in. Instead of sticking to any kind of set bedtime, I usually headed off to brush my teeth and go to bed whenever I was too exhausted to keep reading. That meant I was also too exhausted to pray.

The solution seemed to be to schedule Night Prayer for about a half hour before I conked out, except that I couldn't anticipate the rhythms of my tiredness accurately enough. As long as I was still fully alert, part of me wouldn't concede that it was time for Night Prayer at all. For me, night was differentiated from day not by the absence of light but by the absence of energy. I wasn't willing to call an end to productive day and enter what felt like useless night unless I was sleepy.

During my first Advent as a Catholic, I cast about for a penance or discipline to take on in preparation for the feast of Christmas and wound up giving up some of my "free time" by committing to a bedtime of one in the morning. I deliberately picked a fairly late time, so that the discipline was easy enough that I'd have a chance of sticking to it. If I had picked, say, eleven, going to bed that early might have been such a reach that I would have let myself off of the hook when I lapsed. And besides, the "late" deadline was still a sacrifice: it wasn't unusual for me to be up later than one in the morning several times a week.

Some of my friends were confused that my idea of penance was to sleep more, but what I was giving up was control. A one o'clock bedtime meant that there were external limits on my productive time, that my ability to push myself and punish my body was curtailed.

It also meant I suddenly had a clear deadline for Night Prayer. If I didn't start by about quarter to one at the very latest, I wasn't going to get to say it at all. And if I was going to pray, I really had to get all the other pre-bed business (brushing my teeth, packing tomorrow's lunch) done that much earlier.

The constraints of that Advent season gave me greater freedom through stability. Giving up the (illusory) idea that if I postponed sleep as long as physically possible, I could finish *everything* forced me to set priorities. Before Advent, I had felt selfish or rude if I left a conversation with my roommates when I was tired, but now I could just say, "Sorry, I have to walk away now or I'll break my Advent rule." Limiting my choices freed me from the strain of justifying the need to sleep.

A New Prayer Plan

Unfortunately for my newfound stability, just one month after Advent ended, I moved to California to take a new job, and my entire routine for the Divine Office fell apart.

I had been accustomed to praying Morning Prayer on the subway ride into work, but suddenly my office was within walking distance of my apartment. It took less time to walk there than to say the morning psalms, and I was too self-conscious to finish them in the building's lobby and too bad at planning to start five to ten minutes before I left my house.

To make matters worse, my new job was at a San Francisco start-up, and although the hours weren't unreasonable, they were highly irregular. It was hard to identify any time of day that I could be confident would be free every day of the week. And, as the last straw, I had moved to Berkeley—a college town—in the middle of the winter, and it turned out that rooms pretty much only opened up for rent in September. I spent the first four months of my job moving from couch to couch, unable to set any stable routine for prayer besides trying to get to daily Mass when work allowed.

I kept assuming that my turbulent living situation would be temporary—I never expected to be without a bed for four months—so I postponed sorting out my spiritual life until I had a more stable foundation in my worldly life to build upon. But even after I finally was able to sign a lease, the chaos didn't abate, and organized prayer didn't make it back into my schedule.

I still found time for passing pleasures that were easier to slot in, such as reading and texting with friends, but I continued to omit profound pleasures. I mostly limited even my indulgences to things that could be interrupted, since I kept struggling to find any time I could expect to enjoy as my own, off-limits to anything else. It felt fine to look up from a book, but wrong to stop in the middle of a prayer because of a text or a coworker poking his head in, so I kept defaulting to not starting the prayer at all.

There was probably a better way to address the problem in situ, but the absence of routine, housing, and some of my closest friends left me feeling so rootless in California that I returned to Washington, DC, within a year. That may make me the only person to move to DC because she wanted a more relaxed, grounded life. Once I'd returned home, it was time to figure out a good routine for my daily devotions.

I hadn't succeeded in squeezing prayer into my schedule, so this time I cleared my mental calendar and picked slots for prayer *first*, trusting that the rest of my life would fit into the time that remained. Night Prayer remained hard to schedule, but as I prepared for my next job, I determined that I could reliably reserve time for Morning and Evening Prayer. They would fall on my commute to and from work.

That adjustment has worked out fairly well for me, but my prayer schedule still has a tendency to fall apart on weekends, when I don't commute. I've compromised by committing to saying whichever Hour from the breviary is appropriate when I'm leaving my house and returning to it. If that means on a lazy Saturday that I don't start praying until I leave the house at two o'clock, so be it. I can flip to Mid-Afternoon Prayer and launch into "God, come to my assistance" as I put my key in the door.

Leaving or returning to my house has become a Schelling point, one that has stayed stable across two jobs and four apartments since I moved back to DC. A Schelling point is an idea from game theory; it represents the place where two (or more) players naturally converge if they don't have the chance to communicate ahead of time. When researchers asked subjects where and when they would meet someone in New York if they hadn't been able to communicate anything but the date ahead of time, the answer turned out to be . . .

(Take a second to try to guess.)

". . . under the clock in Grand Central Station, at noon." My inward and outbound commutes offer me a Schelling-stable solution. It's easy for me to default to this "natural" time for prayer.

Divinizing the Daily Routine

Most people pray the Divine Office in moments of rest—standing, sitting, or kneeling—but I like that scheduling these Hours for my commutes means that I wind up praying the psalms while walking. Based on the schedule I've chosen, the Liturgy of the Hours graces the liminal parts of my day, when I transition from one place and role to another. I like saying these prayers when I'm in motion so that they can guide the shift I'm making.

Praying the Liturgy of the Hours during my walk to work divinizes this movement. It highlights the reality that I am making a transition, that there are boundaries between my work and the rest of my life, and that I might bring different disciplines or focuses to each area. Having a ritual for these transitions also makes me feel a bit like a knight putting on armor before battle or a priest vesting for Mass. Because my preparation for work or returning home is prayer, the psalms represent for me a way of invoking God at the outset of a project, just as we invoke him at the beginning of a meal when we say grace.

God is with me always, but praying helps me turn my attention back to him and let his presence shape my actions. Praying the Divine Office right before I begin my next endeavor makes me attentive to whether I'm approaching the project in a way that will help me grow in Christ. I am much less likely to go and be snappish with a coworker immediately after closing my breviary app (after finishing the final blessing) than I am after reading the newspaper on my walk.

Just knowing that I will soon be praying has a similar effect. If something frustrating comes up at work, I don't want to find myself slamming my laptop shut, stomping outside, and then huffing my way through Evening Prayer on the walk home. If I realize that an activity or attitude will interfere with my upcoming prayer, I am more likely to pray right then for help with my anger or fear. Luckily, there are more Hours of the Divine Office available than I can manage to exhaust (only certain orders of vowed religious make a vow to recite all seven prayers daily). So if I do find myself needing a spiritual booster shot, I can pull up the breviary on my phone and begin saying (again), "God, come to my assistance."

Bracketing the Day with Prayer

Although the specific psalms of the Office change daily, the overall structure of the prayers remains the same. The stability of these prayers reminds me pleasantly of the syntax and symmetries of writing computer code.

In most programming languages, in order to get the computer to do something, you have to tell the computer what you're about to do, do it, and tell it when you've finished. So if I were going to write, in pseudocode, the algorithm that tells me that it's time to pray the Liturgy of the Hours, it might look something like this:

```
IF (walking to work OR walking from work):
{
Pull out phone.
Open breviary app.
Pray Liturgy of the Hours.
}
```

The if-statement tells me when the instructions held within the brackets should be executed, and the brackets are what hold all those steps together. Thus, a misplaced bracket can cause big problems, keeping your program from ever going on to the next part of a problem or leaving it stuck in one loop forever. As a result, programmers may not be pushy about other grammar rules, but they tend to be hypersensitive to the symmetry of brackets. One programmer-turned-artist, Randall Munroe, has a cartoon that simply states, "(An unmatched left parenthesis creates a tension that will stay with you all day."[1] I have only a dabbler's experience in programming, but it was enough for me to develop a passionate love for properly matched parentheses. And although I don't run into many in actual computer code, I tend to notice analogous matched pairs in the rest of my life.

Because Morning and Evening Prayer bracket my workday, they serve the same function as the parentheses in computer code. If I only get to say one, something feels *off* about my day. Those prayers are what bind my entire workday together into one module, but they also set it off as a submodule of some larger project.

The more I say the Divine Office, the less I feel I'm interspersing the psalms throughout my day and the more I feel I'm tucking my work, my reading, and my relationships within the prayers of the psalms. These prayers may not be the hardest or the longest or the loudest things I do all day, but they're the reliable things I do every day. They're the punctuation that forms the syntax for all my other choices, the heartbeat thudding quietly and powering all my other activity, the primer on my canvas that prepares it to receive paint.

Bound Together by the Divine Office

This heartbeat of cyclic prayer isn't solitary or purely personal. When I first learned about the Liturgy of the Hours and the way it's recited in monastic communities all over the world, the thought that immediately leapt into my head was "The sun never sets on Catholic prayer."

Whenever I pick up my breviary, it's a near certainty that someone else is mouthing the same words along with me; one time zone over, a nun might have just put her book down; and a priest an hour to my west will pick up the refrain in *his* breviary when I'm done. The song never dies.

And the Divine Office links me not just to other people around the world today, but to myself across time. The psalms in the breviary follow a four-week cycle, so I'm also praying in unison with *myself* one month ago and one month in the future. No matter what else is changing in me or the world around me, the sameness of these prayers links me laterally to other people today and vertically to other moments of identical prayer in my own life.

This cycle offers solidarity and constancy, even as other parts of my life are in flux. I don't know whether I'll hold the same job or be in the same city, but I *will* run across the same prayers in the same sequence. Over time, memories will accrete to my breviary, as moments in my life become tied to particular psalms. When I next come back to that Morning Prayer of Monday, Week One, I may remember the last time I prayed it, where I was, whether it was windy, and what was troubling me.

I have this experience with frequently reread novels, which wind up interleaved with experiences. When I pick up the 2013 copy of *The Year's Best Science Fiction*, I can see in my mind exactly the fire I sat by while beginning it for the first time (and remember how odd it was for a California hotel to have a fire at all, but even more so for the hotel to

have laid one in July). I feel my slight furtiveness as I ducked
out of part of the conference I was attending to read just one
more story, hidden away in the lobby.

As I move through my day, it makes a difference to me
to know that I'll be returning to these prayers and possibly
remembering *this* moment. It makes me feel cared for and a
little more connected to the Communion of Saints, who (like
my future self) are remembering us in the prayers they join
to ours.

The picture of overlaid, harmonized moments of prayer is
very beautiful to this math nerd, who likes to imagine things
sub specie aeternitatis—outside of time, from the perspective
of eternity. All of the Monday-Week-One-Morning-Prayer
Leahs are strung alongside each other, a superposition of
images caught by the blinks of a strobe light. Or I can imagine all of those moments ruched together. Just as a seamstress
bunches a ribbon by dipping a needle in and out along its
length, and then pulling it tight into its final, gathered form,
the repeated Monday-Week-One-Morning-Prayer moments
line up and lie flush against each other, bound together in
symmetry by their common thread of prayer.

Learning Empathy through the Psalms

I find that beauty piercing, but it does tend to draw me up and
away into abstraction. Thankfully, the psalms themselves are
a little more grounded, and they can form the basis for more
concrete bonds of empathy and agape between me and others
in the here and now. For me, a move toward communion with
others sometimes starts with a sense of distance.

When I read the psalms laid out for the prescribed Hour in the Divine Office, there's sometimes a jarring disconnect between the sentiments of the prayer and the way I feel while praying. I might pick up the breviary, still giddy and light-hearted from a good conversation with a friend, and find that the appointed readings are songs of lamentation. Or I might be frustrated, hurt, and lonely when I run across "Upon you no evil shall fall, no plague approach where you dwell" (Ps 91:10, DO) and find myself thinking, "Yeah, right."

As I read through this Hour's psalm, I like to pause to ask, "Who is praying this?" and consider the possibility that the answer is someone other than "me." When I am open to the idea that a psalm may not be speaking directly to my needs and petitions, I frequently find that it speaks to me in a roundabout or unexpected way—often it's someone else's intention that rises to my awareness. If the psalm doesn't match my mood, I may realize that it echoes the joy or sorrow of a particular friend; then I try to offer this Hour of the Office for the intention of that friend and to follow it, if I can, with some thoughtful action.

When the sentiment of the psalm doesn't call to mind anyone I know in the here and now, I might cast my mind back to the parables of the gospels or the people of the Old Testament, and let the passionate words of the psalm shade these scriptural figures with a little more emotion and immediacy for me. These alien-feeling meditations can help me reap a more empathetic understanding of my fathers and mothers in the Faith.

But sometimes the atmosphere of the psalm doesn't match anyone I can think of, living or dead. In those instances, I remember that the cyclic prayers of the Liturgy of the Hours forge connections for me forward in time as well as backward. I can pray for the people to whom this psalm is applicable who remain unknown to me. Perhaps they are already in my life, but I am currently blind to their feelings and circumstances, which is why I cannot connect them with today's reading. Or perhaps I haven't met them yet, but pausing to reflect on this psalm will make me better prepared to receive and love them when we finally cross paths.

When a problem or feeling is unfamiliar to me, it's harder for me to be empathetic, and I can be distant or cold or rude. The psalms and the strong, varied emotions they express are a kind of training for me. I get to encounter, pray for, and try to understand people experiencing unfamiliar needs, joys, and despairs. These textual experiences help me expand my library of sentiments. Having an archetypal example or handle for a particular category of feeling can make it easier to recognize and respond to this genre of feeling in my day-to-day life.

For example, you may have felt *saudade* frequently without ever encountering a name for this feeling. The Portuguese word refers to the love that remains when the beloved person or object is gone, a blend of the pain of absence and the pleasure of having something wonderful enough to miss. But until you learned the word, you might have treated each moment of saudade as isolated and not made a connection between all the different people, places, and objects that trigger the peculiar, pleasurable ache of saudade. Now that they all fit under a common word, it's easier to collect and contrast them, thereby enhancing your understanding of the nuances of this kind of love.

The psalms may not teach me new words, but the specific, vivid expressions of joy or longing teach me new categories of feeling. "Like a deer that longs for running streams, my soul longs for you" (Ps 42:1, DO) is one verse that was particularly novel and suddenly applicable everywhere. Being primed with these specific examples helps me better understand my life and the lives of others.

I do get a great deal of the same benefit from fiction, which takes me inside the heads of other people, but those books don't necessarily teach me how to address God from that position. The Divine Office increases my ability to care *about* other people in my life while also tutoring me in how to care *for* them. The psalms are a truly universal prayer, uttered everywhere at every time. Although individual psalms are particular, addressed to different seasons and sentiments in life, they all share the same orientation toward God.

When I make space in my life for these prayers, they draw me onward and upward toward God and, at the same time, link me to the people walking beside me on their own winding paths to transformation through God's love.

Chapter 6
Lectio Divina

When a friar friend of mine suggested that I try out *lectio divina* (divine reading), I wasn't sure how to begin. Although clearly I could handle the reading part of this practice of prayerful Bible reading, I wasn't sure how to do it prayerfully.

Since I wasn't raised a Christian, my exposure to the Bible had come mostly through excerpts assigned in my Western Civilization class in college or read aloud to me at Mass. Plus, of course, I knew a smattering of pithy phrases, some from the King James Version and some from literary imaginings of biblical events, that had crept into the culture divorced from their context ("By their fruits ye shall know them," "Physician, heal thyself," "Bring me the head of John the Baptist!" etc.). I hadn't ever sat down with the Bible without an assignment or a task in mind. Even after my friar friend broke lectio divina down into its four traditional components for me, I worried that I would need more structure to be able to try it at all.

Classically, the four stages of lectio divina are *lectio, meditatio, oratio,* and *comtemplatio* (read, meditate, pray, and contemplate). The first step, lectio, is simply to read over the chosen passage. Then, in meditatio, the reader thinks about the reading, not in the driven, thesis-oriented way I was used to from writing college papers against a deadline, but in order to clear mental space, allowing the passage to bear fruit in the heart. The goal is not to explain the text but to be changed by it. The third step, oratio, is prayer; after two stages of listening to God speak through scripture, the reader is ready to reply—though the reply is much more likely to take the form of a question or a thank-you than a textual argument. The final stage, contemplatio, is also prayer, but it is less conversational, more a time to pause and rest in God's presence.

Cold Feet

As far as I could tell, the four stages were arranged in order of increasing difficulty, and I wasn't sure I had a handle even on the first. In the ordinary course of events, I read for pleasure or for research, and lectio divina didn't seem to fit into either category. In prayerful reading I shouldn't just tear through the text, drinking in the story on a single pass, the way I did with novels; but on the other hand, I doubted I should approach the passage with the same focused, goal-oriented mentality I used for research. Lectio divina was supposed to help me open myself to God, not encourage me to sift God's word for my own purposes.

Owing to my uncertainty, I kept putting off any attempt at this type of prayer. My most frequent excuse was "I should wait to try this spiritual practice until I know I can do it competently. I wouldn't want to be unfair to lectio divina or to God by not doing it well." Of course, since I wasn't making any progress by avoiding lectio divina, this line of thinking left me on track to finally pick up my Bible around the fourth of never. I was ignoring the second word in the phrase "spiritual practice" and making the great the enemy of the good.

Even after I noticed this flaw in my reasoning, I was still too intimidated to try lectio divina. I didn't want to approach any or all of the four steps badly and somehow wind up being disrespectful. I wasn't yet familiar with this prayer written by the Trappist monk Thomas Merton:

> My Lord God, I have no idea where I am going. I do not see the road ahead of me. I cannot know for certain where it will end. Nor do I really know myself, and the fact that I think that I am following your will does not mean that I am actually doing so. But I believe that the desire to please you does in fact please you. And I hope I have that desire in all that I am doing.[1]

Lacking this encouragement in prayer, I convinced myself that my ignorance was an insurmountable hurdle. I couldn't even try this kind of Bible study *once*, I told myself: since I didn't know how long it would take, I couldn't schedule it. When I tried to picture what praying lectio divina would be like, I kept imagining opening my Bible and going blank, or muddling along unproductively and winding up stuck in a spiral of anxiety about how much I had to do before I was allowed to stop. Luckily, when this visualization revealed to me my specific fear, it turned out to be something I knew how to grapple with.

Saved by the Bell

For my first try at lectio divina, I employed a strategy I'd used in conversation with flesh-and-blood people—I set a timer. In order to be able to leave conversations in a pleasant way (especially at a party), I sometimes set an alarm on my phone to go off in fifteen or twenty minutes and tell my friends what I'm doing. That way, even if I'm having a good time, I have a natural moment to exit, so I can still get to whatever else needs to be done with my evening. And if I'm not enjoying the conversation, I don't need to worry about slighting my conversation partners; I'm leaving based on an arbitrary timer, not in order to escape a particular story or speaker. I hoped God wouldn't mind if I took the same approach with him, to give me the nerve to start a conversation at all.

I set a timer for twenty minutes, promising myself I could close the Bible and stop when it went off, regardless of whether I felt I "accomplished" anything during that period. I couldn't fail the way I framed it. My job was just to spend twenty minutes with scripture: reading, thinking, and praying as I chose; the fireworks were up to God.

I started with the beginning of the Gospel of John. I wanted to start with the beginning of *something*, but didn't want—if I turned out to be reading quickly—to run into Genesis's "begats" on my first time out. So I chose John, since I had heard his gospel was slightly more mystical than the other three—I hoped I might get a little lost in its depth.

John's gospel opens:

> In the beginning was the Word, and the Word was
> with God, and the Word was God. He was in the
> beginning with God. All things came into being
> through him, and without him not one thing came
> into being. What has come into being in him was
> life, and the life was the light of all people. The
> light shines in the darkness, and the darkness did
> not overcome it. (Jn 1:1–5)

I felt the temptation to move quickly, reading for the story and skipping anything confusing, but I made a conscious decision to slow myself down and discover questions to contemplate and meditate upon. To accomplish this aim, I pretended that what I was reading wasn't *quite* in English. When John talks about life, he means something a little different from the set of all beings that grow, metabolize, and reproduce (the definition I'd learned in biology class). Instead of quickly assuming that John meant the same thing I understood by "life," I wanted to pay close attention to what the word meant in this specific context.

Making Reading Harder . . . to Make It Easier

I decided to treat most of the words I read during lectio divina as though they might be "false friends"—foreign words that look like English words but turn out to have a different meaning than you'd expect. For example, *blesser* is a French verb that looks as though it should mean "to bless" but actually means "to wound." I tried not to get too attached to what I assumed John must intend; I wanted to let the text surprise me.

To break my usual casual reading habits, I reached for a technique I'd employed in theater class when I had to scrutinize my lines to understand my character. I looked for a repeated word, like "light," and checked whether the speaker meant the same thing by this word in every instance. In order to check, I tried translating some of the verses into the only other language in which I was semifluent (French); this made me think a lot more about why the (Greek-to-English) translator had chosen that particular English word rather than another.

I looked at the second sentence and wondered whether, if I were translating the Bible from English into French, it would make more sense to say that the Word *était* in the beginning with God or that the Word *a été* in the beginning with God. The first (the imperfect) implies ongoing past action. The second (the simple past) often refers to something that happened once and then stopped. Even a linking verb had the potential to catch my attention and help me ask questions about God's nature.

Another profitable technique I used was to read over a few verses and then close my eyes and try to remember exactly what I'd read. My goal wasn't to memorize the Bible or even the specific verses I was trying to recall. I wanted to see what I flubbed—which part of the reading was least intuitive to me or least likely to stick in my head.

I got this idea from a pattern of mistakes I had made with a voice teacher in high school. In one lesson, after I'd missed a note in "Good Thing Going" for the umpteenth time, my voice teacher told me it wasn't my fault. "There's a reason you keep trying to sing that note," she said. "Stephen Sondheim is a bit of a bastard to singers. He'll spend the whole song making you wait for that note, building it up, drawing out the suspense. Then, when you get there, he doesn't give it to you. You're technically trying to sing the right note, but Sondheim isn't giving it to you yet."

Just as a singer longs for the note that resolves the melody, I expected that paying attention to what I was anticipating when I read a Bible passage would give me a clearer idea of the structure I expected to see under the story. However, my musical intuitions are much sharper than my theological ones. If I misremembered a word or made a substitution when I covered the text, it wasn't necessarily a matter of trying to hit the right note too soon. I might just as easily be exposing some misunderstanding I had of God, which led me to expect the wrong sort of resolution or to perceive a tension where none existed.

Computer scientists use a similar strategy of learning through mistaken predictions to train machine learning algorithms. Their programs make predictions, check them against real-world data, and then modify themselves and try again. As a computer encounters errors and revises itself, its progress resembles that of a blindfolded person struggling to find her way up a hill. Robbed of sight, she has to gauge which direction is uphill from the feeling of the slope under her feet. If she follows the rule "Go in whichever direction feels like up," she will make some wrong turnings and may even wind up short of her goal (the edge of a ridge may feel like the highest point around, even if it's short of the summit), but she's likely to at least find herself away from the lowest points of the valley.

I didn't have anything as tactile as the slope of a hill or as precise as a dataset to guide me when I studied scripture, so I relied on my recall-and-repeat trick as a way of forcing my errors out into the open, where I could interact with them. It turned out I was in good company—when I dove deeper into the history of my Faith, I found that theologians had been learning through mistakes long before the first learning algorithm was coded.

Once again, I had the chance to learn from my mistakes, drawing on the traditions of *via negativa* or *apophatic* theology. On a very large hill, you can't see enough of the slope to be able to proceed unerringly in the right direction, even if your eyes are uncovered. God is much larger than the means we have to perceive him, so instead of trying to look at him in order to move toward him, sometimes we can get farther by looking at what he is *not* and moving in the opposite direction. At its most basic, *via negativa* includes simply using negative definitions of God. We're all familiar with finite, limited things, so it is easier for us to understand that God does *not* resemble them in being finite than it is for us to understand exactly how God is infinite.

We don't know what perfect love looks like, but we have plenty of experience with lapses in charity, and we know that God never wrongs us in the way we wrong each other and ourselves. Each lapse in love, just like each bounded, finite quality we observe, tells us something about who God is, if only that he is *different* from the latest insufficiency or limitation manifested in our present world. By moving away from everything that is *not* God, we can back our way toward him up that hill, where we can see more clearly by being nearer to his light.

When I try to force out contrasts and expose my own anticipations during lectio divina, I want to discover what in my vision of God is not like God, and to improve my model accordingly. A computer corrects itself using the error-checking data provided by its creator; the divinely inspired Bible provides the information I need for self-correction. It is an article of faith that any true understanding of God must be compatible with the wisdom we were handed in the scriptures. God can't be entirely contained in the Bible, but he is consistent with it. When my fill-in-the-blank exercises strike a false note during my lectio, I know I have a concern to lift up in prayer during the oratio.

Speaking an Incarnational Language

Some of my errant anticipations were fueled less by bad theology than by cached thoughts. The most common way I err is by adding King James phrasings into the Catholic translation I'm reading. Since I didn't grow up with the Bible or Mass, I most frequently encountered its language in aphorisms, plays, and historical fiction (a character's Christianity might be indicated by his "Thees" and "Thous").

When I started going to church, I was surprised to find that the Catholic Church had a different text; even if the translation was more accurate, it felt aesthetically "off" to me. The archaic language of the King James Version differentiated it from all the other texts that I encounter in my daily life. It seemed right that the Bible should be somehow set apart. I sympathized more than a little with the narrator of Terry Pratchett's novel *The Truth* who fears that a printing press, with its swappable words and letters, will muddle language and meaning: "But if you took the leaden letters that had previously been used to set the words of a god, and then used them to set a cookery book, what did that do to the holy wisdom? For that matter, what would it do to the pie? As for printing a book of spells, and then using the same type for a book of navigation—well, the voyage might go *anywhere*."[2]

When I hit phrases I recognized in the Bible, it was easy for me to get distracted from the text in front of me. For example, when I read Second Samuel, I couldn't help thinking of the plot of Orson Scott Card's *Ender's Shadow*, the first place I'd ever seen "My son, my son, Absalom. Would God that I could die for you."[3] I enjoy making connections, but I kept thinking the Bible was alluding to the texts it had actually informed because of the order in which I'd read them. (In just the same way, *Frankenstein* seemed clichéd when I first read it, since I had already read so many works inspired by it). Since I was more fluent in and familiar with the novels and quotations I already knew than with their scriptural sources, it was easy for me to find my thoughts straying.

To take my mind off language differences and literary allusions, I turned to a new language. At the Mass I attend, an interpreter standing just below the altar translates the Mass and the readings into American Sign Language (ASL) for the benefit of deaf parishioners. I've dabbled in the study of the language and knew just enough to be able to follow along a little and pick up new signs from context.

Because I'm a beginner in ASL and seldom get the chance to practice with a language partner, most of the words I've seen signed live are ones I encountered first at church. As a result, ASL feels slightly divinized to me, as perhaps Latin did to people who grew up in the Church before the Second Vatican Council. Because each sign is marked a little by the place I first learned it, ASL practice or signed conversations in secular contexts remind me of prayer.

It would be impossible for modern English to become divinized for me; I've been speaking it for much too long to find many new words to associate with the divine. The ones I do discover through church ("supersubstantial bread," "hypostatic union") tend to be jargon, words I won't encounter again in the secular world. But "world" itself is a sign I'm most used to seeing in the context of "Lamb of God, you take away the sins of the *world.*" When I go to use the sign for "world" outside of church, muscle memory brings the entire Agnus Dei to mind, just as my fingers itch to type an *e* every time they strike out "th."

When I watch the interpreter, it's a bit of a strain to keep up, even though I'm hearing the corresponding words from the lector or the priest. But I find it helpful to struggle a bit during Mass. Nothing that's being said is so simple or quotidian that I can afford to listen casually, and it's actually a lot easier to learn and retain information if you have to struggle a little to make it out. Researchers have found that students remember more of articles they read that are printed in a difficult-to-read font than of those that are legible and easier to scan.[4] I wouldn't want to read the Bible in six-point Comic Sans font, but watching ASL turned out to be both hard and enjoyable for me, and it also makes it easier for what I see and hear to enter my heart and make a home there.

Since ASL helped me so much at Mass, I tried to carry it over to my private scripture reading in lectio divina. Sometimes when I read, I try signing whatever words I know in the verse I'm reading. It turns out to be much harder for me to *sign* "mercy" casually than to read the word casually. The sign for "mercy" uses both of my hands. My hands are open, fingers relaxed, middle fingers slightly curved in. I hold my hands up in front of my body, fingers pointing up, and move them downward twice or so, as if drawing forgiveness down from above. Ever since I learned how to sign the word, this movement has seemed like the embodiment of Portia's description of mercy to Shylock in *The Merchant of Venice*:

> The quality of mercy is not strain'd,
> It droppeth as the gentle rain from heaven
> Upon the place beneath: it is twice blest;
> It blesseth him that gives and him that takes.[5]

Using the sign rather than the word forces me to consider that gentleness, since I enact it myself—my hands move smoothly and slowly, not jerkily or abruptly. The grammar of ASL also makes me think about "him that gives and him that takes," since changing the object of a verb means a change in the orientation of my body. If I want to talk about my offering mercy to you, my palms will face you while I sign. When I sign about God's mercy to me in the Kyrie, my palms face my own body as I softly indicate the mercy moving from God above me to fall upon my head.

Even if I don't know the signs for all the verbs I encounter in lectio, thinking about how I'd need to shift my body to indicate who is doing what to whom helps me pause, reflect, and learn. ASL is the way I've found into this kind of deep reading, but I imagine there are a wide variety of approaches, even diagramming sentences, that would keep any phrase from passing too quickly and lightly before the reader's eye.

Translating Words into Action

The gospels and epistles are themselves a work of translation: the disciples who recorded them translated experience into history to give their readers some sense of the Incarnate Word through the same kind of ordinary text that records mundane history. In this, as in all good things, they took their cue from Christ.

When Jesus taught his followers, he used parables and analogies drawn from everyday life. To explain forgiveness and humility, he told the story of the prodigal son, who demands his inheritance, squanders it, returns home weak and regretful, and is still welcomed back as a son (Lk 15:11–32). Christ's stories are close enough to the daily lives of his listeners to be recognizable, but there's something jarringly discordant about them. The prodigal son is welcomed back without punishment or anger. The workers who came late to the vineyard receive a full day's wages from the overseer. The dishonest steward is rewarded for defrauding his master in order to forgive the debts of his neighbors (see Mt 20:1–16; Lk 16:1–13).

Christ is teaching his listeners a new language of action using the tongue they currently know. The stories start in familiar ways, but their conclusions make it clear that Christ is proclaiming something new and different. The parables don't reach the resolution that Christ's followers would expect from their own lived experience.

The hearers' (and readers') experience to date isn't rich enough for them to be able to receive instruction in this new language of action through study and stories alone. Thus, when Christ comes, he doesn't testify just with words, but with his whole life. In his essay collection *Open Mind, Faithful Heart: Reflections on Following Jesus*, Pope Francis explains that, as Christians, our witness must be like that of Jesus—not limited to spoken and written words. "When fully accepted, the epiphany of God becomes flesh

in the life of the disciple in such a way that it can be transmitted only from this 'incarnation.' That is to say, it can be
transmitted to others not by words of flesh and blood, not
by human wisdom, but only by the scandalous inevitability
of the cross; it can be transmitted only by *martyrion*, by
bearing witness."[6]

Christ uses his own life and the invented lives of the people in his parables to reveal more than he could with words
and argument alone. Sometimes he has to tell a story more
than once, drawing his hearers slowly toward understanding.
When Christ describes the kingdom of heaven in the parable
of the weeds among the wheat, the disciples follow him and
ask him to explain the story because they did not understand. Christ clarifies part of the metaphor but immediately
follows it with three new parables with which the disciples
must struggle (see Mt 13:24–50).

He has told them a story they do not understand, and a
painful awareness of their own confusion drives them back
to Christ to ask for help. Although in this moment they feel
most ignorant, they have already learned something about the
limits of their knowledge; struck by their own insufficiency,
they return, as Peter says they must: "Lord, to whom can we
go? You have the words of eternal life" (Jn 6:68).

If Christ had explained the kingdom in a way that completely satisfied the disciples, they would have come away
with a graver misunderstanding that would preclude seeking
correction. It is important for the disciples (and me as a reader
today) to understand that, despite our study, the kingdom
remains slightly foreign to us; our fluency with the fallen

world leaves us struggling to discern and imitate heaven's dialect.

The goal of listening to Christ, whether in person as the disciples did or through lectio divina as I do, is not simply to hear or even to be able to understand well enough to explain to others, but to be changed. Lectio divina culminates in contemplatio because all study of Christ is ultimately directed toward the imitation of Christ. Success will come not through my own furious efforts, but through clearing a space for Christ to speak and me to hear.

In order to be ready for contemplatio, I depend on habits such as translation to give me a sense of the largeness of Christ's revelation. When I finish my lectio and move to meditatio and oratio, I want to be sure that I have questions to offer in prayer. The questions themselves aren't always particularly weighty, but they help me train the good habit of turning to God and asking him to teach me, rather than standing at a distance and trying to study him on my own.

By the time Paul writes his first letter to the Corinthians, he has learned enough from the witness of Christ's life to remind his brothers that their understanding is not complete:

> For we know only in part, and we prophesy only in part; but when the complete comes, the partial will come to an end. When I was a child, I spoke like a child, I thought like a child, I reasoned like a child; when I became an adult, I put an end to childish ways. For now we see in a mirror, dimly, but then we will see face to face. Now I know only in part; then I will know fully, even as I have been fully known. (1 Cor 13:9–12)

The full truths that Christ expressed incarnationally, that the disciples recorded, that the scholars translated, and that I wind up fumbling with in lectio divina are beyond my ability to completely understand. I'm as bad at imitating Christ, moment to moment, as I was at mastering the tones of Mandarin when I visited Beijing after a one-week crash course in the language. Apparently my pronunciation of the word "popsicle" barely sounded like a word at all, but when shopkeepers listened very charitably, they usually assumed it to be a very mangled attempt at "trash can." I could make only so much progress when people tried to help me and correct my errors; I often couldn't even hear the difference between two tones, let alone reproduce the right one reliably. In the same way, sometimes I can't even conceive of what the Christlike response to my circumstances would be; the right action is too far away from my usual fluencies for me to master.

Studying scripture through lectio divina is like a moral vocabulary drill. It reminds me of choices I could have been making and tutors me in the lexicon of loving acts. The more fluency with scripture I pick up, the more natural it feels to try to translate some of my everyday life into its prophetic terms.

Speaking Scripture in My Secular Life

When I started studying ASL, I sometimes practiced the few signs I knew when someone happened to use the corresponding English word in a conversation. It helped me connect the sign for "book" to actual physical books and to the kind of sentences in which "book" turned up. If I only used the sign during my ASL practice, the word seemed to belong only on a flash card.

Similarly, I didn't want the scripture I read to stay confined to lectio divina or the readings at Mass. But just as it took a while before I ever used ASL spontaneously, it took several years of exposure to the Bible before a verse came to mind in what I might call the secular part of my life and I started to experience the fruits of a little scriptural fluency.

I had gone with friends to see Joss Whedon's horror film *The Cabin in the Woods*, and as the credits rolled, I had an unsettled feeling I couldn't put a name to, a discomfort that wasn't just a reaction to the blood and gore. Then, without my looking for it, an Old Testament verse just rang out in my head: "Why do you spend your money for that which is not bread, and your labor for that which does not satisfy?" (Is 55:2).

I could tell that line explained my unease before I was able to translate it into ordinary English and figure out why. I had loved *Buffy the Vampire Slayer* and other witty Whedon productions. On *Buffy*, all that cleverness is in service to the story of Buffy and her friends growing in love for one another and relying on that love to save the world from vampires, giant snake demons, etc. In *Cabin*, however, the bonds between friends are more tenuous, and even the central friendship turns nihilistic: the two main characters choose each other over saving the world and don't seem too troubled by what they sacrifice.

Isaiah's words came to me because Joss Whedon was using his considerable talents to tell an outwardly attractive, airy confection of a story that looked like proper food but wouldn't nourish a viewer the way *Buffy* and his other shows had. If I hadn't had Isaiah to rely on, I might eventually have reached for the next best phrase in my vocabulary, "bait and switch," but Isaiah's phrase was richer and more true for the situation.

A generic bait and switch might involve a triviality (seeing a photo of a friend with a celebrity and later discovering it was actually taken with a wax figure). But Isaiah is writing about something essential to life that we neglect while glutting ourselves on something entirely inappropriate. My new language showed me this important distinction between the trivial and the essential very clearly.

When I engage in lectio divina, I try not to chase after insights during my study but to think about the practice as sowing the seeds for new connections such as the one I made between Isaiah's exhortation and the horror movie's message. The more I'm steeped in scripture, using whatever techniques I can come up with to engage with it deeply and avoid skimming, the more often it will feel natural to view the choices I make and the circumstances I face through its lens.

I may not be fluent in its lessons, but even a fumbling familiarity with scripture can be enough to help me notice when I am confused and prompt me to turn to prayer and reflection to address my confusion. Just as using ASL and memory exercises forced me to notice the inconsistencies between my anticipations and Christ's actual words, embracing biblical parallels shines a spotlight on the inconsistencies between my thoughts and acts and the inspired words of the Bible. And then, as always, I can thank God for even partial knowledge, face my error, and back at least one deliberate step away from *this* mistake. Then I begin again.

Chapter 7
Mass

I started attending Mass with my Catholic college boyfriend shortly after we started going out. It was part of an exchange: every time I went to a Mass with him, he went to a ballroom dance class with me. During the two years we dated, especially at the very beginning, I was intensely attentive to the Mass.

It wasn't because I was reverent. I was terrified.

I had never entered any kind of church or place of worship before (except for the year we all turned thirteen and I went to see some of my middle school classmates sing their haftarah at their bar or bat mitzvot). Everything was foreign to me, and I was sure that my unfamiliarity with Catholic traditions would leave me standing or singing at the wrong moment, somehow offering a grave insult or disruption to my boyfriend and his fellow parishioners. Every Sunday, I would make sure to sit up perfectly straight, trying to anticipate and imitate the actions of the people around me, feeling as though iron bands were tightening around my chest.

Margaret Mead at Mass

As the weeks passed and my anxiety dissipated, I began to experience a different kind of focus. I felt like an anthropologist or someone watching a *National Geographic*

documentary, filling in my own David Attenborough nar-
ration in my head. Well, possibly I was a bit snottier than a
real wildlife observer, but my tone was usually the product
of distance rather than contempt.

If you narrate anything literally and seriously enough, it
tends to sound absurd, and the audio playing in my mind as I
observed and analyzed tended to sound something like "The
priest dips his water-flicking device into his bucket and casts
water over the audience in surprisingly long arcs. He does
not sprinkle every parishioner one by one; rather, by moving
and flicking regularly, he generates an approximately uniform
probability of being blessed."

My use of the word "audience" in my internal voiceover
betrayed the fact that I saw the whole ritual as performative
rather than participatory. But I like the theater, and if I was
going to be going every week, I wanted to learn more about
what was being staged. So rather than focusing so much
on the scripture readings and the homilies, I became more
interested in the structure of the rituals and traditions that
surrounded them.

I kept alert during Mass because I was trying to notice
and retain whatever confused me so I could follow up on it
later with the priest or with my friends or on my blog. I was
like a student on her summer abroad whose most frequent
question is "What is the English word for *x*?"

As I did more reading and asked more questions, I had
the orderly pleasure of seeing the pieces start to fit together.
Chasuble, alb, maniple—learning the words drew my attention to specific subcomponents of the priest's vestments, so
that I no longer thought of him as one vaguely medieval mass

of fabric. Having words for each individual garment let me pose specific questions and learn how each piece was meant to reflect and further the aims of the liturgy.

I was learning a new language through immersion and tutoring, and I wanted to see what it could express. A computer programmer learning a new language would cement her new knowledge by putting it through its paces; to find out what was different about this new tongue, she would rewrite in this new syntax some programs she already knew well. What was easier to say? What suddenly required many more caveats to express clearly? What choices were suddenly available? Pioneering computer programmer Alan Perlis advised that "a language that doesn't affect the way you think about programming, is not worth knowing."[1]

Most of us have some experience with the kind of mental shift a new language can afford even if our experience comes from spoken languages, not programming languages. When I started studying foreign languages, I was surprised to find that most languages let you draw a distinction between a formal and an informal "you" in a way that English does not. The choice in French between *tu* and *vous* lets me address people with greater precision, but also means that I am forced to evaluate, whether deliberately or unconsciously, my level of intimacy with my interlocutor before I open my mouth. The Matsés language spoken in Peru requires its speakers to note the source of any claim they make: its grammar differentiates between events you witnessed yourself and those you heard about secondhand as cleanly as English separates present and future tenses.

I tried to cultivate the same curiosity about Catholic ritual that I would have about any new language, whether programming or natural. What new emphases did it create? How would it change the way I think?

The Calendar of Salvation

The first such structural difference I noticed in the visual language of Catholicism was the liturgical calendar. Just as I can't help but notice whether an acquaintance *tutoyers* me (addresses me informally in French), I couldn't help but notice the color of the priest's vestments and the way they matched any wall hangings or altar cloths inside the church. Once I had a fumbling grasp of this language, it was impossible to be in dialogue with the Church and remain unaware of what kind of day it was.

If, in the middle of a stretch of green Ordinary Time days, the priest suddenly emerged in red, I knew it was the feast day of some martyr, and I had the opportunity to ask about who was being celebrated and why. The burst of pink that blooms on Gaudete and Laetare Sundays in the middle of the long periods of penitential purple in Advent and Lent alerted me that something different was afoot, even before I knew those days had special names.

After I graduated from college, and even before I converted, the liturgical calendar helped give shape to my life. Previously, the academic calendar had subdivided my weeks and months into semesters and exam periods, fitting them into a narrative with rising and falling action. In the adult world, where people work year-round at the same office every day instead of having different classes on different days, it was hard to keep track of the passage of time.

The liturgical calendar traces out the salvation story of the gospels. The somber air of Lent hints at the darkness and fear from which we are delivered through the miracle of Easter: the rising of Christ. That story is so central to the Faith that it's echoed on the other side of the calendar at Advent when we go through the same process on a smaller scale to celebrate the entrance of Christ into the world at Christmas. In both seasons, the penitential period reminds us how badly we need Christ and teaches us to call him Savior by reminding us what he freed us from.

The feasts of holy martyrs and saints, sprinkled throughout the year, show us an incredible diversity of ways to answer God's call to love each other as he loves us. The feasts of the saints make the great sweep of the year's salvation story concrete and human-sized.

A Christ-Centered Coordinate Plane

Each individual Mass replays this narrative of salvation, as well as playing its part in the story that stretches over the year. The readings from the Old and New Testaments show us how to live, and the crowning moment of the Mass, the Eucharist, is our lesson in *why* we want to live in union with God.

In the liturgy, we remember our own sins and the pain they caused us and our neighbors, shortly before we receive Christ in the Eucharist, saying, "Lord, I am not worthy that you should enter under my roof, but only say the word, and my soul shall be healed." Once again, we have a little Lent, a moment of penance, to prepare us for the magnitude of the gift we are about to receive. Catholics and the Orthodox are divided from most Protestants because we assert that the Mass is more than just a dramatic reenactment of Christ's sacrifice, done "in remembrance of" him. We believe that in the Eucharist we receive the fullness of Christ's death and resurrection. When the priest snaps the wafer, Christ consents to be broken again for our sake, in order to make us whole. This is why we are here. Everything else in the Mass is there to prepare us for that moment.

When I started attending Mass as an atheist, I was skeptical about transubstantiation, but I tried to understand, in theory, what it would mean for the Eucharist to actually be Christ's sacrifice, not just a symbol of it. In order to make sense of Communion, I wound up drawing from my study of topology rather than theology.

Imagine that wherever you walked, you traced out your path behind you, maybe with ink, maybe with string. There would be some places where the only evidence of your passing was a single, lonely line, but other locations (the threshold of your front door, perhaps) would show a thick mass of overlaid lines. Every point where lines cross would be a location that you occupied more than once. The *times* at which you stood there may have varied, but the *position* would remain the same. If, instead of leaving behind a line, you left behind a shadowy figure of yourself, these crossing points would be occupied by superimposed copies of yourself, like a multiply exposed photograph.

If you wanted to set numbers to this scenario (and I usually do), you could think about tracing your walks using the

(x, y) system of Cartesian coordinates, noting the latitude and longitude of your position from moment to moment. Every instance of overlap would be a set of two or more times you stood at the exact same (x, y) spot. Your last trip to your old high school might be separated from your next visit by a period of five years, but as long as the latitude and longitude remained the same, an intersection would exist with respect to space, if not time. If you wanted to be able to tell the difference between [you leaving your apartment this morning] and [you the day you moved in], both of whom stood at the same (x, y) spot in front of your door, you'd need to add a third variable, t, to keep track of time and expand your coordinate system to (x, y, t) accordingly.

When I picture all the instances of myself, graphed and identified in this fashion, I have other tools besides just keeping an eye on the clock to distinguish between all those different versions of myself. Just as all the Leahs standing at the same (x, y) in front of my door occupy the same place, even if we visit that spot at different moments in time, all the Leahs walking alone anywhere can be said to occupy the same condition with respect to the company we're keeping. No matter the x, y, and t, wherever and whenever I am alone I have the same value for a new variable we'll call A, which equals one when I'm alone and zero when I'm not.

Essentially, I can think of myself as doubled back and overlaid whenever one part of my circumstances has repeated itself.

I thought of the sacrifice of the Mass as being an example of the same kind of singularity. Throughout history, wherever they were in space and time, Catholics have continually doubled back to intersect in this one space. The location of the church might change [different (x, y)] or I might turn up for a different Mass (different t) from week to week, but in the long chain of coordinates that describe me, there's one variable that remains absolutely the same at every Mass. In the expanded system of (x, y, t, C), C equals one when I am in the presence of Christ-made-flesh, and zero whenever I'm not. At Mass, during the liturgy of the Eucharist, I'm always in the exact same position *with respect to Christ's sacrifice* regardless of whether I'm in the same location in space and time (x, y, t) as his Crucifixion.

In fact, I'm also in the exact same place with respect to Christ as everyone else in the church. If I add on a variable N for name at the front of the coordinate system I've been making up, I have a way to distinguish myself from anyone else who is in the same church at the same time. What's more, the coordinate system (N, x, y, t, C) is sufficient to describe and differentiate all the members of the Body of Christ worshiping in Christ's presence at Mass in all times (past, present, and future) and all places. We are different people kneeling in different places and times, but among all the coordinates that describe each one of us one is constant: C equals one for us all because we are all in the presence of Christ's Body and Blood.

If I picture my life unspooling like a reel of film, Mass is the moment when all of these strands loop back and layer themselves on top of each other, twisting around to join each other like the fancy ribbons on top of Christmas presents. Any individual strand might loop very far out before it returns back to the crowd of souls clustered at the Mass, but whether you go to church every single day or have just wandered back through the doors for the first time in years, there's a radical equality in our shared position. Every person's C-coordinate equals one, exactly the same as everyone else's, as long as they've turned up in Christ's incarnate presence.

A Syzygy of Saints

This superposition isn't limited to the living. When I go to Mass, I'm standing before the same Presence that hung over John and Mary when they wept at the foot of the Cross, or that Saint Dominic lifted high for his brother monks to see when he celebrated the Eucharist, or that Saint Tarcisius shielded with his own body and life from the mob of Romans who tried to tear his Body out of that small saint's embrace. These saints may be much more kind or holy or brave than I am, but we share some kind of fellowship standing in the presence of the same Person, albeit in different times and places.

The Mass is part of what makes the Catholic Church small-c catholic, or universal. It lets all of humanity congregate at the feet of God together, even during our time on Earth, making sure that, no matter how our times or we ourselves change, no matter what values our (x, y, t) coordinates take on, there is *one* thing we can always experience in common with our fellow parishioners: our unity before God.

Of course, there are many other universally shared variables. I could talk about myself relative to (x, y, t, E), where E equals one if I'm currently on Earth and zero otherwise. My value of one for E unites me with every person who has ever lived (though maybe not everyone who *will* live). Astronauts may have periods of E equals zero, but they've all had *some* moments of E equals one to share in common with me.

So why is unity before God more important than unity upon Earth or unity as hominids or any other unity I could come up with? Because the *syzygy* (a nearly straight-line configuration of three celestial bodies) isn't trivial for me. It's true that there are many other qualities (such as having DNA or being shorter than twenty feet tall) that bring me into alignment with the whole human community, but being in the presence of Christ is different. That variable doesn't merely describe my physical location or attributes. It describes whether and how I am loved. Sharing love with someone else is a much closer bond than sharing a hairstyle or an age.

The Mass brings us all into alignment through the relationship we share with God. When I struggle to love someone, I can remember that, no matter how many of that person's characteristics rankle me, we share God's love for us in common. Our lives lie tangent to each other with respect to that great love, so we're never entirely separate. I can call on God himself to help me love my neighbor as he does; or I can turn to the saints for tutoring, reaching along the one thing I *know* we have in common, to draw closer to them and to ask their help in changing some of my other variables—those that describe my will and capacity to love—to match theirs.

A Scary Sacrament

I kept trying to translate the Mass in this way, to find a way to understand these foreign rituals by analogizing them to the mathematical frames of reference I already knew and loved. As I sought to expand my knowledge, I couldn't help but be drawn into all the nerdy, logistical details related to the Eucharist.

For example, if the priest dropped a consecrated host, he would pick it up and eat it himself, rather than leave it on the ground. If a host did have to be discarded, it had to be first dissolved in water and then poured onto the earth (not into the sewer system). These rules reminded me of the detailed laws setting limits on how you could display and dispose of the American flag.

However, for all the attention paid to the treatment of Christ's corporeal gift *before* you consumed it, I seldom heard Catholics talking about what happened to the consecrated bread and wine after we ate and drank it. It was a little hard for me to reconcile the rather bestial and bodily process of chewing and swallowing with the extreme reverence displayed for the Eucharist when it was outside the body.

I'm not alone in being thrown by the mechanics of consuming Christ. When Jesus told his disciples that they would have to eat his flesh and drink his blood to live fully, they were repulsed (especially since Christ used a rather low word for "eat" that could also be translated as "gnaw"). The disciples turned to each other in consternation and said, "This teaching is difficult; who can accept it?" (Jn 6:60).

However, in considering it undignified for Christ to be physically integrated into my body, I was, unintentionally, flouting the mysterious gift of the Incarnation. There *was* something odd about God becoming flesh, but if he had already chosen to humble himself to be born with a body like ours and to live and die like us, who was I to be the one to withdraw from physical communion? If Christ chose to accept a physical body, how could I turn up my nose at his offer to mingle his body with mine?

Even though I had already considered the implications of the Eucharist as an observer trying to better understand Catholicism, it wasn't easy to come to terms with it as a convert. As I prepared for Baptism and reception into the Church, I was more than a little terrified of receiving Christ in a much more personal and deliberate way than when I simply bowed my head for a blessing at the end of the Mass.

In the course of managing all the worldly, logistical aspects of my conversion, I had to find a way to explain the Eucharist. Plenty of the friends and family who were coming to my Baptism were not Catholic and many were atheists, so I sent out a big Baptism FAQ e-mail ahead of time to try to spare them being caught unawares in church as I had been during my first few months of Masses. I summarized the steps of the liturgy, putting off explaining Communion until the last question in the e-mail. When I got to it, slightly overwhelmed by the task, I ended up writing:

> The final sacrament received is the *Eucharist*. For some sects of Christianity, the central point of their worship is the homily, when the priest/reverend/etc. interprets scripture. For Catholics and Orthodox (and some Lutherans and Anglicans) the whole point of the Mass is not Bible study but direct contact with the risen Christ, fully present in the Eucharist. This is probably not the best metaphor, but think of it as the good version of the moment in *Lord of the Rings* when Frodo cries out, "I am naked in the dark, Sam, there is no veil between me and the wheel of fire! I begin to see it even with my waking eyes."[2]

Um, except here you have all that intensity, except the Person you're face-to-face with is infinitely good, and instead of a burning ring, it's the Beatific Vision, and, y'know, there's a reason I'm not in charge of catechesis.

Christ Changing Me from the Inside Out

To make this sacrament a little more comprehensible to my friends, I reached for literature. For myself, I found my thoughts drifting to an old thought experiment, dating back to the Greeks. In his *Life of Theseus*, set down back in the late first century, Plutarch writes:

> The ship wherein Theseus and the youth of Athens returned from Crete had thirty oars, and was preserved by the Athenians down even to the time of Demetrius Phalereus, for they took away the old planks as they decayed, putting in new and stronger timber in their place, in so much that this ship became a standing example among the philosophers, for the logical question of things that grow; one side holding that the ship remained the same, and the other contending that it was not the same.[3]

Bit by bit, the entire ship was replaced so that not a single board or nail of the original remained. The philosophers couldn't come to an agreement about whether, at the end of this process, it could still be said to be Theseus's old ship. I had liked debating this question with friends in my philosophy section, but the problem of the Eucharist took this paradox out of the realm of abstraction.

I see myself in the position of Theseus's ship when I take Jesus into my body under the outward appearance of food, something I normally digest and incorporate into myself. Some part of me is being replaced, or at least augmented, by divine grace.

When I approach the altar to receive the Host, I am still weak and enslaved to sin. The Eucharist carries grace to me, enters my body, and strengthens and straightens my corrupted will, just as a workman might pry a warped board out of a hull to replace it with freshly planed wood. Once a repair is made, I am free to choose whether to take good care of the patch or to treat it in the same nonchalant way that allowed the original panel to become warped. I am changed by contact with Christ in the Eucharist, but in order to benefit fully, I have to choose to honor that change.

Wherever I am, I can always invite Christ into my life and ask him to fill me with more of his strength and his light, but the outward sign of the sacraments is especially powerful for me. It's easier for me to engage in spontaneous, ejaculatory prayer when those pleas are the continuation of something that began at Mass. It's the difference between asking Christ to help starting now, and asking him to *keep* working within me, helping me to accept and cooperate with the gift of himself that he offered to me earlier this day or this week at Mass.

The transformative power of grace received through bread and wine reminded me of a Chinese legend about *mellified men*—mystics who were transmuted entirely into honey, whose golden corpses were reported to be a powerful medicine. To begin the change, the men of this legend would bathe in honey and eat only honey, becoming so saturated that their sweat and tears would pour forth in the form of honey. After they died, these men were supposed to be buried in honey-filled tombs, in which their transformation into crystallized mummies would be completed. If such a process actually existed, you would still be able to recognize friends who had undergone it, since they would have become perfectly lifelike honey statues.

The mellified men go through a more extreme process of replacement than that of the ship of Theseus. Instead of having a series of replaceable parts swapped out, their flesh and bone is replaced by a foreign substance. However, even as their flesh and bones are replaced, something of their identity remains in the shape of their crystallized body.

Meditating on the legend of the mellified men helped me understand the incredible diversity of the saints. Each of the saints is united wholly to God: in him they move and live and have their being (Acts 17:28). And yet, communion with God is not a great annihilation. We are not dissolved into God, so diluted by his infinite nature as to be erased. Somehow, our unique souls are preserved.

It is feasting on the Eucharist that allows us to be transmuted, rather than blurred out. C. S. Lewis writes in *Mere Christianity* about this kind of growth in God: "There are no real personalities apart from God. Until you have given up your self to Him, you will not have a real self. Sameness is to be found most among the most 'natural' men, not among those who surrender to Christ. How monotonously alike all the great tyrants and conquerors have been, how gloriously different are the saints."[4]

G. K. Chesterton picks up the theme in *Orthodoxy*: "It is true that the historic Church has at once emphasized celibacy and emphasized the family; has at once (if one may put it so) been fiercely for having children and fiercely for not having children. It has kept them side by side like two strong colors, red and white, like the red and white on the shield of St. George. It has always had a healthy hatred of pink."[5]

Somehow, the mixing of man and Christ makes everyone sharper and more distinct, instead of yielding some averaged-out blandness. The saints have been perfected and healed while still remaining recognizably themselves. These holy men and women have been steeped in Christ the way the mellified men were immersed in honey, so that they retain their own shapes and souls, even as they are transfigured by what they eat and breathe.

The legendary mellified men eat, drink, and bathe in honey, which is sweet and lovely but ultimately inert. Although the honey preserves their bodies, it cannot preserve their lives. The men turn into beautiful corpses, but they are still corpses. In contrast, the saints are sustained by the living Christ, who is Life and Love itself, made flesh so that we may consume him directly. Some saints, like Catherine of Siena, were even granted the grace to be sustained *solely* by the Eucharist for periods of their lives. When they are wholly filled and changed, the saints are *more* alive than they were in life, since they are finally fully joined to the great I AM.

At the end of this sea change, they have become something rich and strange, but they are only strangers in that they are more vibrantly, blindingly themselves than ever before. Just as you might feel oddly out of place in your own bedroom after you'd finally tidied it up and set it to rights, we on Earth, as part of the living Church Militant, are easily startled and confused by the glory of the Church Triumphant. We're not used to seeing people so clearly.

There is one other resemblance between the mellified men and the saints. After their death and transformation, the honey mummies were intended to be medicine, such potent medicine that a piece of their transfigured flesh could, according to legend, heal broken limbs and other ailments. The bodies of the saints also offer healing to those around them, but the graces that flow through them cannot be exhausted or used up. The saints serve not as mere tinctures but as servants of God, bearing us up with their work and prayers.

For me, this is the resolution to the ancient paradox of Theseus: the grace present in the Eucharist alters me, but it does so by making me more myself. Like a mellified man, I find that I am changed by what I consume, but the holy food distributed at Mass brings me healing and eternal life, not just sweetness in death.

The grace poured out in the Mass—and in all the prayers the Catholic Church has offered me—helps me to grow in this new life, altered and yet still myself. Every day, God's love tutors mine.

Conclusion

Trusting Christ as Peter Does

When I was received into the Catholic Church, I had the opportunity to choose a Confirmation saint. I figured that it might be a good idea to choose a saint who was personally familiar with the errors I was prone to commit, so I picked Saint Augustine, who, just like me, was a former gnostic (someone who elevates the abstract to the point of ignoring or despising ordinary human interactions). But if I had been looking for a patron saint of general errors, I might have chosen Saint Peter. I've since adopted him as the unofficial patron saint of my prayer life, since I feel I can trust Peter to teach me the right disposition toward error.

Before Peter makes his three famous *denials* of Christ (see Lk 22:54–62), he has already been stumbling through his service to his teacher. Reading the gospels, I was fascinated by Peter's three *contradictions* of Christ—his enthusiastic attempts to follow his teacher so closely that he accidentally runs on ahead and has to be pulled back onto the right path by Jesus. In the storm-tossed boat (Mt 14:22–33), at the Transfiguration (Mt 17:1–8), and during the prelude to the Last Supper (Jn 13:2–8), Peter misinterprets Christ and requires correction.

131

Despite these struggles, Peter is the disciple chosen to become first among the disciples, the rock upon which Christ establishes his Church. I wonder if Peter was chosen not for being the most perfect among the disciples (John is the beloved disciple to whom Christ entrusts his own mother) but for being the one who was most willing to bring his imperfections to God for correction.

It should be reassuring to us that Christ chose a man who struggled in discipleship to lead his Church. A man who started at sainthood would be a strange model for the Church as a whole; the Body of Christ is certainly composed of sinners who follow Christ haltingly, with our hearts often divided. But if we can't trust ourselves to know Christ perfectly —as even Peter could not—how are we to follow him?

Flailing toward Christ

In the gospels, Peter tends to fail by flailing. Once he's gotten in over his head, he keeps struggling, trying to find some way to make sense of the situation. Usually his troubles are theological—he is trying to digest Jesus' hard teachings and difficult parables. But when Jesus walks on the water, Peter wrestles with both understanding and faith, and it places him in physical danger.

> Immediately he made the disciples get into the boat and go on ahead to the other side, while he dismissed the crowds. And after he had dismissed the crowds, he went up the mountain by himself to pray. When evening came, he was there alone, but by this time the boat, battered by the waves, was far from the land, for the wind was against them. And early in the morning he came walking

> toward them on the sea. But when the disciples saw him walking on the sea, they were terrified, saying, "It is a ghost!" And they cried out in fear. But immediately Jesus spoke to them and said, "Take heart, it is I; do not be afraid."
>
> Peter answered him, "Lord, if it is you, command me to come to you on the water." He said, "Come." So Peter got out of the boat, started walking on the water, and came toward Jesus. But when he noticed the strong wind, he became frightened, and beginning to sink, he cried out, "Lord, save me!" Jesus immediately reached out his hand and caught him, saying to him, "You of little faith, why did you doubt?" When they got into the boat, the wind ceased. And those in the boat worshiped him, saying, "Truly you are the Son of God." (Mt 14:22–33)

Hearing this passage read aloud at Mass corrected a misunderstanding I'd had about the story for a long time. I'd always incorrectly remembered that Jesus summons Peter to come out of the boat to meet him, choosing this particular act of faith as a test. But clearly it is Peter who proposes the adventure, asking Jesus to command him.

Like Benedick in *Much Ado About Nothing*, Peter needs some way to express his love, and at this moment, he could well have delivered one of Benedick's lines: "Come, bid me do any thing for thee."[1] Christ had already bade Peter to do something for him when he said, "Do not be afraid," but longing either for a more difficult challenge or for a more visible act of obedience, Peter asks for another task. Unfortunately for Peter, he finds himself in the same position as

Benedick: what is asked of him proves to be beyond his power to perform.

I've frequently heard priests, in their homilies on this passage, say that Peter's faith was weak, or that he fell prey to doubt, but it seems to me that they sell Peter short. Peter is sinking in the middle of a storm, with every reason to fear for his life, but, as Samuel Johnson put it, the prospect of death concentrates the mind wonderfully, and Peter's mind concentrates on Jesus Christ.

Sinking in the middle of waves whipped up by a strong wind, Peter cries out, "Lord, save me!" Instead of trusting in his own strength, Peter reaches outward, holding on to his faith that there is only one direction worth traveling—"Lord, to whom can we go? You have the words of eternal life" (Jn 6:68). That faith is enough for Peter to be saved, in the sea or on the land.

When I'm lucky, I live like the disciples in the boat in the storm—prone to fear and doubt but held safely. Frequently, though, I wind up like Peter, overextended and floundering. Once he is stuck, Peter doesn't try to take charge and undo his mistake; he keeps flailing his way toward Christ. My prayer life often feels like this kind of thrashing in Christ's general direction, waiting and trusting that he'll reach across the gap I can't close on my own.

Failing Out Loud

Before I started sourcing my lessons in failing fruitfully from a Jewish fisherman, I took them from a Jewish teenager. In E. L. Konigsburg's *About the B'nai Bagels*, her protagonist, Mark, recruits his brother Spencer to help him prepare for his upcoming bar mitzvah. As part of the ceremony, Mark has to chant his haftarah (an excerpt from the Old Testament) and is self-conscious about his weak singing voice. Once Mark sings through his assigned section, Spencer gives him the following advice:

> "I have only one word of advice to give you."
>
> "Give already."
>
> "That word is *fortissimo*. . . . It's Italian for *loud*. When in doubt, shout. That's what I'm telling you."
>
> "I should shout? Everyone will hear for sure how bad I am."
>
> "But, my dear brother, if you sing loud and clear, it will be easier on the audience. You're making it doubly hard on them. Hard to listen to and hard to hear."[2]

I read this passage when I was in elementary school and, to the betterment or detriment of the people around me, tried to live by Spencer's advice, which is the complete opposite of the oft-repeated aphorism "Better to remain silent and be thought a fool than to open your mouth and remove all doubt." The lucky thing was that loud fools tended to get fixed.

In my high school choir, I wasn't the only girl who had a tendency to go flat on a descending series of notes or to have my pitch waver when singing close harmonies, but I think I was the only one to be called out and corrected for it in almost every class period. Many of my classmates were a good deal better than I was (I have one parent with perfect pitch, and one who is tone-deaf, and thus I can't complain too much about being merely serviceable), but when the other girls did run into trouble, they had a tendency to sing quietly, to make sure they wouldn't be *heard* being wrong.

I lowered my volume at concerts if I hadn't managed to master the part by then, but I tried to remember that rehearsals were low stakes, where nothing too terrible would happen if I hit the wrong note and was called to the piano to try the phrase. When my teacher had me sing the problematic measure *a cappella*, plunking the correct note on the piano while I was still holding my pitch, I sometimes even aired the causes of my errors *fortissimo*.

"Can you *hear* that you're flat, Leah?"

I was tempted to—and for a while did—give the "correct" answer: "Yes." But, as classes went by without my actually learning how to correct myself, I started fessing up and admitting that I *could* hear that I wasn't on the note being played, but that, once I was fairly close, I couldn't tell whether I was flat or sharp, because the different timbres of my voice and the piano key made it hard for me to notice small differences in pitch within that range.

I never did wind up correcting my faulty pitch, but I wouldn't have had a chance at it if I hadn't put my errors on gaudy display. As I went on through life—in math class, in ASL class, and just in conversation—I used *fortissimo* as my rallying cry. *Fortissimo* spurred me to volunteer to be first to do the problem on the board, to perform an example dialogue in front of the class, or to just pipe up and say, "I don't know that reference. Could you expand that sentence into a paragraph, please?"

As I began learning about my new faith, I assumed Peter must have been the *best* of all the disciples, since Jesus chose him as the first pope and foundation of the Church. Instead, I found, he seemed to be the one among the Twelve who let his nascent faith ring out *fortissimo* even when he struck a wrong note, thereby drawing the correction he needed (and we need) from the Lord.

Offering the Wrong Sort of Hospitality

I disrupted my chorus class, but Peter's *fortissimo* was strong enough to interrupt God and his prophets. At Christ's Transfiguration, when he is exalted in God's light and attended by the great Jewish prophets, it is Peter alone, among the three apostles in attendance, who speaks up—and winds up erring.

> Six days later, Jesus took with him Peter and James and his brother John and led them up a high mountain, by themselves. And he was transfigured before them, and his face shone like the sun, and his clothes became dazzling white. Suddenly there appeared to them Moses and Elijah, talking with him. Then Peter said to Jesus, "Lord, it is good for us to be here; if you wish, I will make three dwellings here, one for you, one for Moses, and one for Elijah." While he was still speaking, suddenly a bright cloud overshadowed them, and from the cloud a voice said, "This is my Son, the Beloved; with him I am well pleased; listen to him!" When the disciples heard this, they fell to the ground and were overcome by fear. But Jesus came and touched them, saying, "Get up and do not be afraid." And when they looked up, they saw no one except Jesus himself alone. (Mt 17:1–8)

There's an incredible contrast between Christ's Transfiguration and Peter's prosaic offer. Christ shines out amid the uncreated light, and while the other disciples are awestruck, Peter inserts himself into the conversation between Christ, Moses, and Elijah in order to ask if they need somewhere to stay and if he could possibly help. Before Peter can finish speaking, he is overshadowed by the voice of God, who redirects the disciples to the heavenly matters before them, preventing them from being distracted by Peter's earthly considerations.

Again, I frequently hear harsh assessments of Peter's error here from the pulpit; homilists warn me not to ape Peter by trying to hold too tightly to God or reducing him to the point where I can contain him. In this reading of Peter's exclamation, Peter offered housing to Christ and his companions in order to hang on to the vision being granted to him, to extend it for longer than it was being offered. He tried to "immanentize the eschaton," to shrink heaven's glory until it is small enough to fit into our earthly lives, with no concern for what must be pared away.

This shrinking and concretizing of God is a common human temptation, well described by C. S. Lewis in his *Screwtape Letters*. The book is written as a series of instructional letters from a senior demon (Screwtape) to a junior tempter (Wormwood). The letters put forth various methods of diverting and frustrating every feeble human effort to seek God. Screwtape writes:

> I have known cases where what the patient called his "God" was actually located—up and to the left at the corner of the bedroom ceiling, or inside his own head, or in a crucifix on the wall. But

whatever the nature of the composite object, you must keep him praying to it—to the thing that he has made, not to the Person who has made him. You may even encourage him to attach great importance to the correction and improvement of his composite object, and to keeping it steadily before his imagination during the whole prayer. For if he ever comes to make the distinction, if ever he consciously directs his prayers "Not to what I think thou art but to what thou knowest thyself to be," our situation is, for the moment, desperate.[3]

There is a kind of error that looks like Peter's and certainly resembles that of Wormwood's victim, in which one allows the fear of losing hold of God to crowd out the grace of simply being with God. Peter, if granted permission to raise tents, might have become like Martha, focused intently on the things that matter least, justifying a scrupulous attention to worldly detail because the project is technically meant to serve God.

To me, Peter's offer seems more absurd in the moment than acquisitive. Heaven opens, the spirits of the dead appear, and you offer to build shelters? And yet Peter's desire to show hospitality to the prophets does have precedent: at the Passover meal, it is traditional to set a place, fill a glass, and open the door for Elijah. Now, if Elijah were to walk in, it would still be strange to immediately start making up the guest bed for him. We've done our part in preparing, and if he deigned to arrive, the next move would be his. At that point, we're off script—our haggadah (Passover seder instructions) provides no further guidance.

Left to improvise, Peter wants to give what he can immediately, without waiting for direction. In this moment of transcendent change, Peter can only fumble with the mores and laws he has grown up with. Overcome with wonder, he tries to offer *something* to his Lord and these heavenly guides.

In this, Peter almost resembles a cat, the kind who keeps bringing in dead mice and lovingly laying them across his master's shoes. He is determined to offer the best gift he can find, but his experience and capabilities are badly mismatched to the project of pleasing the person he wants to serve. Still, the gift is motivated by love (albeit confused). Unlike the cat, Peter is capable of understanding correction.

Peter's actions at the Transfiguration remind me of another unexpected gift offered in the gospels. When Jesus is teaching in the Temple, he witnesses the people of Jerusalem making their offerings to God. "And He looked up and saw the rich putting their gifts into the treasury, and He saw also a certain poor widow putting in two mites. So He said, 'Truly I say to you that this poor widow has put in more than all; for all these out of their abundance have put in offerings for God, but she out of her poverty put in all the livelihood that she had'" (Lk 21:1–4, NKJV).

The widow has almost nothing, but she is happy to offer everything she does have, with no shame about her poverty. Peter suffers not from material poverty but from spiritual poverty—compared with the gifts and knowledge of Moses or Elijah, let alone Christ, Peter has almost nothing. Nevertheless, he longs to offer what he has for the glory and delight of God, even if in his fumbling he can only imagine offering material gifts.

The widow is unusually poor in Jerusalem, but when it comes to spiritual gifts, Peter is unusually rich among men. He was chosen by Christ to leave his nets and become a disciple; he is drawn aside for fuller explanations of the parables that leave the disciples and other hearers confused. Growing in love for Jesus, he is the first to recognize him as the Christ.

But even having all these gifts, Peter still has only a mite to offer back to God in thankfulness for all the care and correction he has received. God's response to Peter's small offering is to make a larger one in return: he speaks to Peter twice. God speaks first from the heavens, confirming for Peter and the other two disciples that they are indeed following God, and clarifying that there is only one gift that he desires from them, that they listen to the Son he has sent.

For Peter, and for each of us, the words of Psalm 51 hold true: "For in sacrifice you take no delight, burnt offering from me you would refuse; my sacrifice, a contrite spirit. A humbled, contrite heart you will not spurn" (Ps 51:16–17, DO). God no longer asks to be sheltered in the tabernacle Moses built at his command, but for us to allow him to make his home in our hearts.

The second time God speaks to Peter after his outburst, it is Christ who gives Peter the gift of this command: "Get up and do not be afraid" (Mt 17:7). Peter is asked to stand and persevere, rather than retreat or be repulsed by his own inadequacy.

Peter knows now that his sole job is to listen to God. If he does so, then his *fortissimo* errors will be corrected through his close communion with the Son of God. If Peter withdraws in fear, he will be separated from God and alone with his errors.

Overshooting the Mark

In Peter's third contradiction of Christ, he demonstrates the humility and willingness to learn that allows him to persevere after his errors at sea and on the mountain. However, his response to correction still tends to contain the seeds of new errors, which must be corrected in turn.

At the Last Supper, when Jesus bends down to wash the feet of the disciples, Peter is as confused and uncomfortable as I was the first time I attended a Holy Thursday service at which all of the parishioners had their feet washed. At the time, I wasn't yet considering conversion, and I was very reluctant to accept any gift from the Catholic Church when I had no intention of offering anything in return. I did not want to be in debt to the campus church, and I took my scrupulous anti-dependency to the point of never eating any of the snacks laid out after the Masses I attended with my boyfriend lest I receive anything to which I was not entitled as a *real* member of the community.

Peter has no such reason to hold himself apart, but as far as I could tell from scripture, he is similarly concerned with propriety and proportionality. As John tells us:

> During supper Jesus, knowing that the Father had
> given all things into his hands, and that he had
> come from God and was going to God, got up
> from the table, took off his outer robe, and tied
> a towel around himself. Then he poured water
> into a basin and began to wash the disciples' feet
> and to wipe them with the towel that was tied

> around him. He came to Simon Peter, who said
> to him, "Lord, are you going to wash my feet?"
> Jesus answered, "You do not know now what I am
> doing, but later you will understand." Peter said to
> him, "You will never wash my feet." (Jn 13:2–8)

Even though Jesus offers a measure of reassurance, acknowledging that Peter would find his service perplexing, Peter holds to what he knows and thus rejects the gift that Jesus is offering, worried that it is somehow improper.

It's clear that Peter's withdrawal is the result of misinformed love, unlike my own desire to remain apart, because when Christ makes it clear that foot washing is a prerequisite for full communion with him, Peter immediately submits— and then overcompensates:

> Jesus answered, "Unless I wash you, you have no
> share with me." Simon Peter said to him, "Lord,
> not my feet only but also my hands and my head!"
> Jesus said to him, "One who has bathed does not
> need to wash, except for the feet, but is entirely
> clean. And you are clean, though not all of you."
> For he knew who was to betray him; for this
> reason he said, "Not all of you are clean." (Jn
> 13:8–11)

Peter acts as zealot, but he holds on lightly to each act of zealotry, ready to relinquish it if his teacher commands it. When he makes his loud errors, they are not *fortissimo* because Peter has irrevocably committed himself to them but because he has committed himself entirely to Christ. Therefore he offers each act of service, even the misguided ones, with his whole heart.

Tacking toward God

At the Last Supper and elsewhere, Christ and Peter sometimes seem to be playing a game of "Warmer/Colder." Jesus
realigns and guides Peter in the right direction, but although
he is quick to turn around at every "colder" he hears, Peter
then strikes out in a new direction with such gusto that he
tends to overshoot the mark, requiring yet another course
correction. Because Peter progressed in this way, I can trust
that God is patient with my own efforts and that, no matter
how many odd, dead-mouse kinds of prayers I bring to him,
he will correct me and strengthen the love that drove me to
offer *something*.

Perhaps Peter was elevated not *despite* his errors but
because of them. Because he clung to Christ even in his
moments of uncertainty and confusion, he learned the most
from the Teacher he followed, which prepared him to teach
others in turn.

In matters secular and religious, teachers tend to fall prey
to the *expert's fallacy*. They forget which parts of the subjects
they are teaching are hard for beginners and also forget that
their students don't share their habits and heuristics. Mystics can offer us visions of God granted to them through a
singular act of grace, but only those who have been students
themselves, struggling and erring, remember what it was like
to get to know God the hard way, as Peter did, and know how
to teach beginners. His experience made him well suited to
lead the Church.

Peter learned well because he wanted to be open to Christ
more than he wanted to conceal his errors. When I am fright-
ened of a new prayer practice or feel self-conscious about

speaking to God, I try to imitate his *fortissimo* faith. It kept Peter from ever needing the warning given to the Church at Laodicea: "I know your works; you are neither cold nor hot. I wish that you were either cold or hot. So, because you are lukewarm, and neither cold nor hot, I am about to spit you out of my mouth" (Rv 3:15–16).

Error is inevitable as I continue to grow in faith, but if I can persist in Peter's wholehearted, hot devotion to Christ, I will not be spat out—I will be corrected with love by the Source of all love.

Reader's Guide

Whether you are reading *Arriving at Amen* for your own personal enrichment or as part of a group discussion, the following questions are intended to help you get the most out of what you have just read (or to anticipate the themes of the book you are about to read).

Introduction: Chasing Truth as Javert Does

1. One of the unique features of this book is the surprising ways Leah connects spirituality with literature and art as well as the more "left-brained" disciplines of math and science. Have any sources that are not explicitly religious shaped your spiritual life?

2. Leah introduces Inspector Javert from *Les Misérables* as an example of someone whose determination to follow the rules ultimately leads to his destruction. Leah identified with his character, yet her love of order and morality ultimately led her along a very different path. What themes or characters from literature have resonated with and guided you? Are there characters you've loved but grown past?

3. "Do unto others twenty percent better than you would expect them to do unto you, to correct for subjective error." How can Linus Pauling's principle be applied to personal relationships? To work? To the spiritual life?

4. Leah was drawn to the Catholic Church after reaching the conclusion that "morality just loves me," that the existence of moral law implies a loving, attentive lawgiver. This in turn led her to get to know him better through Catholic prayer practices. In your experience, how do faith and reason work together to lead us closer to God?

1. Petition

1. Leah initially resists the idea of petitionary prayer as an exercise in futility. "An omniscient God must know before I did what I wanted (and whether I should have it). I hated people cluttering up my time and attention to inform me of what I already knew." What does she conclude is the point of praying, if God already knows what we need? Is there anything you would add to this?

2. Leah talks about using fictional characters as intercessory icons who call to mind categories or groups of people for whom she can intercede. What or who are some of your favorite intercessory icons?

3. "I can trust Mary to behold me and the person I'm struggling with and to love us both." How does your relationship with the saints infuse your prayer life and help you get outside yourself? What are some ways you've experienced God "untying the knots" in your life?

2. Confession

1. "The Sacrament of Reconciliation is an oddly private grace." Although Catholics are obligated to go to confession and receive the Eucharist once a year, there is a

wide range of personal practice in how often to receive these sacraments. If you were mentoring someone new to the faith, what advice would you offer about this?

2. Leah later continues, "If I let a long time pass between visits to the confessional, putting off the sacrament until I commit a mortal sin, the venial sins I've committed become fuzzier and more indistinct in my memory and feel less consequential. However, that doesn't free me from their effects; the people I've slighted or scorned are still hurt, and the distance I've opened up between my conscience and my actions makes it harder for me to repent, learn, and make amends." How does the simple act of going to confession help us to "repent, learn, and make amends"?

3. The gilded imperfection that characterizes the Japanese art form of *kintsugi* illustrates for us the beauty that God can bring from brokenness. How have you experienced this in your life?

3. Examen

1. Although examen overlaps somewhat with confession, Leah shows that it is actually an act of intentional daily encounter with God. She explores the five steps of examen: Express gratitude. Ask for light. Review the day. Confess. Anticipate the day ahead. Which of these steps come most easily to you? Which do you need to work on?

2. Leah quotes *The Presence of God*, in which the sculptor works the stone first with crude tools and then with

increasingly delicate implements to create the final work of art. How does this illustration speak to you?

3. In the latter part of the chapter, Leah describes taking examen to the next level, with an outward rather than inward focus. Why is this shift in focus an important spiritual development?

4. Rosary

1. How, if at all, does the Rosary factor in to your prayer life right now? When are you most likely to offer this prayer? Do you identify with Leah's early experiences with this Catholic prayer practice?

2. Leah uses the Hail Mary as a circuit breaker to turn her thoughts to God in the midst of temptation to spite or resentment. Is there a prayer practice you can or do use as a circuit breaker in order to disrupt an ingrained bad habit?

3. Do you have a favorite set of mysteries, or do you always follow the traditional order (Joyful on Mondays and Saturdays, Sorrowful on Tuesdays and Fridays, Glorious on Wednesdays and Sundays, and Luminous on Thursdays)? Which is your favorite mystery, and why?

5. Divine Office

1. Although praying the Divine Office (Liturgy of the Hours) is a requirement for Catholic clergy and religious, many "regular" Catholics also find it a helpful way to incorporate prayer systematically into the day. Based on

Leah's description, which aspects of the Divine Office do you find most appealing, and why?

2. Leah's commute turned out to be one of the most stable parts of her day, and a good anchor for a daily prayer practice. What parts of your daily routine remain the same day to day? Are any of them a good trigger for praying the Divine Office or building any other prayer habit?

3. How does the shared reading of Divine Office facilitate a sense of connection with the whole Church as the Body of Christ?

4. What is the benefit of looking at life *sub specie aeternitatis* (outside of time, from the perspective of eternity)?

Chapter 6: Lectio Divina

1. Have you ever practiced the ancient devotion of lectio divina (the slow, prayerful reading of scripture)? How did you get started, and what benefits have you derived from this practice?

2. Which of the four stages (read, meditate, pray, and contemplate) comes most easily to you, and which do you think you most need to develop? What books or other resources have you found helpful in cultivating this practice in your life?

3. Talk about a time when you felt that the scriptures were "speaking" directly to you. How did you translate that "word" into action?

4. Leah set a time limit to help her muster the courage to try out lectio divina. Is there a prayer practice that has attracted you but seemed too hard even to attempt? Is there a way you can set a limit so that it feels less intimidating to start out with?

7. Mass

1. Can you (or have you spoken with someone who can) relate to Leah's experience of attending her first Mass ("I was terrified.")? In retrospect, what do you think are some of the most common sources of discomfort, and what can parishes do to be more welcoming?

2. Can you think of a time when the significance of the Mass as an atoning sacrifice was particularly meaningful to you? A time when you found it difficult to connect in a meaningful way to what was happening? What did Leah's observation about Cartesian coordinates say to you about the nature of our relationship with Christ in the Eucharist and to the worshipers receiving him with us?

3. What did the illustration of the honey-saturated "mellified men" suggest to you about the transforming power of the Eucharist?

Conclusion: Trusting Christ as Peter Does

1. What does it say to you that Jesus made Peter—the apostle who failed the most repeatedly and spectacularly in scripture—the first pope?

2. What does Peter's "flailing" say about our own ability to connect with Christ? How does this relate to Leah's admonishment "When in doubt, shout"?

3. How does learning to trust Christ like Peter help us arrive at "Amen"?

4. What are the most important things you've discovered about yourself and your own prayer journey through reading this book?

Notes

Introduction: Chasing Truth as Javert Does

1. Claude-Michel Schönberg, Alain Boublil, Jean-Marc Natel, and Herbert Kretzmer, *Les Misérables*, with Colm Wilkinson and Terrence Mann, recorded 1987, 1990, compact disc.

2. Victor Hugo, *Les Misérables* (New York: Penguin Group, 1987), 210.

1. Petition

1. Schönberg et al., *Les Misérables*.

2. Shakespeare, *Twelfth Night*, act 2, scene 2, http://shakespeare.mit.edu/twelfth_night/twelfth_night.2.2.html.

2. Confession

1. Leslie Jamison, "Grand Unified Theory of Female Pain," *VQR* 90, no. 2 (Spring 2014), http://www.vqronline.org/essays-articles/2014/04/grand-unified-theory-female-pain/.

3. Examen

1. Shakespeare, *Macbeth*, act 1, scene 7, http://shakespeare.mit.edu/macbeth/macbeth.1.7.html.

2. Jennifer Fulwiler, "Saint's Name Generator," http://jenniferfulwiler.com/saints/.

3. Shakespeare, *Much Ado About Nothing*, act 2, scene 3, http://shakespeare.mit.edu/much_ado/much_ado.2.3.html.

4. Anselm Moynihan, *The Presence of God* (Dublin: St. Martin's Apostolate, 2002), 17.

4. Rosary

1. C. S. Lewis, *The Lion, the Witch and the Wardrobe*, The Chronicles of Narnia (New York: Harper Collins, 2009), 19.

2. C. S. Lewis, *The Last Battle*, The Chronicles of Narnia (New York: Harper Collins, 2009), 185.

3. *The Wizard of Oz*, directed by John Patrick Shanley (1939; Los Angeles: Metro-Goldwyn-Mayer, 1999), DVD.

4. Augustine, *The Confessions of St. Augustine: Modern English Version* (Grand Rapids, MI: Revell, 2008), 14.

5. Divine Office

1. Randall Munroe, "Unmatched Left Parenthesis," *xkcd.com*, http://xkcd.com/859.

6. Lectio Divina

1. Thomas Merton, *Thoughts in Solitude* (New York: Farrar, Straus and Giroux, 1999), 79.

2. Terry Pratchett, *The Truth* (New York: Harper Collins, 2009), 37.

3. Orson Scott Card, *Ender's Shadow* (New York: Tor, 1999), 454.

4. Connor Diemand-Yauman, Daniel M. Oppenheimer, and Erikka B. Vaughan, "Fortune Favors the **Bold** (*and the Italicized*): Effects of Disfluency on Educational Outcomes," *Cognition* 118, no. 1 (2011): 111–15, http://web.princeton.edu/sites/opplab/papers/Diemand-Yauman_Oppenheimer_2010.pdf.

5. Shakespeare, *The Merchant of Venice*, act 4, scene 1, http://shakespeare.mit.edu/merchant/merchant.4.1.html.

6. Francis, *Open Mind, Faithful Heart: Reflections on Following Jesus* (New York: Crossroad, 2013), 134.

7. Mass

1. Alan Perlis, "Epigrams in Programming," http://www.cs.yale.edu/homes/perlis-alan/quotes.html.

2. J. R. R. Tolkien, *The Return of the King*, The Lord of the Rings (Boston: Houghton Mifflin Harcourt, 2012), 916.

3. Plutarch, *Life of Theseus*, trans. John Dryden, http://classics.mit.edu/Plutarch/theseus.html.

4. C. S. Lewis, *Mere Christianity* (New York: Harper Collins, 2009), 227.

5. G. K. Chesterton, *Orthodoxy* (New Jersey: J. P. Piper, 2014), 101.

Conclusion: Trusting Christ as Peter Does

1. Shakespeare, *Much Ado About Nothing*, act 4, scene 1, http://shakespeare.mit.edu/much_ado/much_ado.4.1.html.

2. E. L. Konigsburg, *About the B'nai Bagels* (New York: Simon and Schuster, 1969), 83.

3. C. S. Lewis, *The Screwtape Letters*, in *The Complete C. S. Lewis Signature Classics* (New York: Harper Collins, 2002), 195.

Leah Libresco is a blogger for Patheos and also works as a statistician in Washington, DC. She is a 2011 graduate of Yale University, where she earned a bachelor's degree in political science.

In 2012, Libresco was featured on media outlets ranging from CNN to EWTN when she announced on her blog, *Unequally Yoked*, that she was converting from atheism to Catholicism.

Libresco, a Mineola, New York, native, previously worked as an editorial assistant at the *American Conservative*. She also has served as a curriculum developer, research associate, and research analyst. She has appeared on CNN's *American Morning*, and *CNN Newsroom*, as well as National Public Radio, *The Drew Mariani Show*, *Unbelievable with Justin Brierley*, WOR's *In the Arena*, and *A Closer Look with Sheila Liaugminas*. She has also contributed to *The American Conservative*, *First Things*, and *The American Interest*.

AVE

AVE MARIA PRESS

Founded in 1865, Ave Maria Press,
a ministry of the Congregation of
Holy Cross, is a Catholic publishing
company that serves the spiritual and
formative needs of the Church and its
schools, institutions, and ministers;
Christian individuals and families; and
others seeking spiritual nourishment.

For a complete listing of titles from

Ave Maria Press

Sorin Books

Forest of Peace

Christian Classics

visit www.avemariapress.com

AVE MARIA PRESS
Notre Dame, IN
A Ministry of the United States Province of Holy Cross